designing Water gardens

A UNIQUE APPROACH

conran
OCTOPUS

First published in 1999 by

Conran Octopus Limited

a part of Octopus Publishing Group

2–4 Heron Quays

London E14 4JP

www.conran-octopus.co.uk

ISBN 1 84091 156 5

Colour origination by Sang Choy International, Singapore

Printed in China

Commissioning Editor: *Stuart Cooper*

Editor: *Helen Woodhall*

Editorial Assistant: *Alexandra Kent*

Copy Editor: *Sarah Sears*

Art Editor: *Alison Barclay*

Picture Research: *Helen Fickling*

Production: *Julian Deeming and Zoe Fawcett*

Index: *Helen Snaith*

Captions

Page 1: *The curving tree trunk and hanging blossoms in this formal pool contrast with the severe geometry of the hard landscaping, creating a dramatic composition. Larger trees need to be rooted in the ground, smaller ones may be planted in an enclosed container within the pool.*

Page 2: *Formal falls can be decorated in many ways. Here, the mosaic waves rise up towards the real water, which is pouring down in a single clear fall into the pool.*

Page 3: *Drops of water decorate a beautiful water lily.*

contents

introduction

The beloved Sun Mother, spirit of life and light, decreed that a period of darkness should follow light so that the earth's creatures could rest and refresh themselves. She soared up into the heavens to leave the earth without her light. The water spirit, who inhabited the springs, streams and lakes, rose in anguish to follow her, but unable to reach her in the heavens, fell back to earth, weeping with exhaustion, showering flowers, trees and grass with crystal droplets. This is how an ancient Aboriginal myth of creation explains the phenomena of rain and dew, and is just one of many myths, legends and stories that have been inspired by water.

Water in nature travels in a continuous cycle. Lifted from the oceans and lakes by the sun's energy, it is condensed into clouds. Falling to earth again as rain, some soaks through the earth until it reaches a layer of non-porous rock. Forced from here to the surface where it emerges as a spring, the trickle becomes a stream or brook, and then a river, which follows a course to its destination, be that a lake or the sea. It is this cycle that underlies the structure of this book, each chapter looking at a different stage – the Source, the Course, the Outlet and the Destination. These identify the characteristics of water at each stage, and examine how best to exploit them in your garden.

Water's face is constantly changing expression, making it endlessly fascinating. Even before the rain falls we can watch the clouds forming. Beautiful white cumulonimbus tower up through the haze of a sultry afternoon. A highly charged atmosphere and hushed expectancy mark the approach and onset of a big thunderstorm.

above: *Rain, drizzle, dew or even the garden sprinkler can leave sparkling beads of water on leaves.*

right: *Art Nouveau jewellery? Looking at this picture of water droplets falling from a leaf it is easy to see how designers are inspired by nature.*

We become aware of a disturbance in the air, a low and threatening distant rumbling, the air becomes oppressive and, with a surprising suddenness, the rolling leading edge of the black storm cloud is upon us and the first heavy raindrops start to fall. Rain like this after a long, dry spell brings with it a delicious smell of sweet freshness.

Fog and mist, on the other hand, are perhaps the gentlest sources of water. They create an enclosed and mysterious world where visibility is reduced to unexpected looming shapes that appear close at hand and then are just as suddenly gone. Great drops slowly form on leaves, twigs and branches before dripping to the ground. This state is almost constant in the high cloud forests of the Andes, and plants thrive there, as in a perpetual mist propagator. Then there is the steady rain that comes in autumn, when we like to lie snugly tucked up in bed, listening to it beating on the window pane. Strong winds blow the trees and shake cascades of drops onto the earth below. This is steady, useful rain; it sinks in and recharges the aquifers, raises the water table, and fills the reservoirs.

In winter, water changes its complexion more radically, becoming snow and ice. When it starts to snow, the flakes fall in abundance, sometimes lazy and feathery, sometimes blowing diagonally or even horizontally from leaden clouds. They are always moving, hypnotic to watch, pausing in mid-flight to dart upwards abruptly before being driven down again in great gusts. Snow is a wonderful insulator, protecting tender plants and small creatures. After it thaws, the moisture seeps into the earth, providing a slow release of water throughout the spring.

opposite: *Sculpted by warm winds, the sun and tides, glaciers take on fascinating shapes as they pour fresh water into the ocean.*
below left: *Heavy rains hammer maple leaves, saturating the soil and stimulating growth.*
below centre: *Hoar frost makes these rushes resemble regiments of icy spearheads pointing upwards in the cold, still dawn.*
below right: *Heavy cumulus clouds build up against the sun. If they develop into cumulonimbus a thunderstorm will follow.*

The life blood

Water is central to all life. Sixty-five per cent of the human body is water and most of the chemical reactions that occur within the body require it. You could survive for weeks without food but only a few days without water. When we cry, salt water springs from our eyes; when we sweat, water seeps from our skin to cool us; and, faced with the prospect of a delicious meal, our mouth waters. Water has always been vital to the survival of mankind and since ancient times, man has settled near water. The Egyptians depended on the water of the River Nile for drinking water, for irrigation, as a line of communication and for recreational purposes. A remarkable degree of precision in water management was achieved in those early times. Devices were perfected to measure the rise and fall of the river (nilometers), giving advance warning of fluctuations in water levels. Water was channelled through narrow canals and often lifted to a higher level for irrigation by means of the *shaduf,* a counterbalanced beam and bucket. The importance to agriculture of efficient irrigation systems was indicated by Homer in the *Odyssey (c.* 800 BC) when he describes the gardens of King Alcinous (one of Odysseus' hosts on his travels):

> Two plenteous fountains the whole prospect crowned,
>
> This through the garden leads its streams around,
>
> Visits each plant and waters all the ground.
>
> Whilst that in pipes beneath the palace flows
>
> and thence a current on the town bestows.

The Romans too built canal systems to move water around the country and, where the topography demanded, incorporated vast tunnels and aqueducts. In 312 BC Appius Claudius built the first aqueduct, the Aqua Appia, to supply water to Rome. By AD 226 no fewer than eleven aqueducts carried water into the city.

Water is much more to us than just a practical and physical amenity that fulfils our basic needs. It is an irresistible magnet for young and old alike. Why are we so drawn to water in all its forms? Why has it always held such an enduring fascination for us? The merest sight or sound of water has always been enticing – a tranquil pool glinting through trees or the distant roar of a waterfall will invariably tempt us to wander off our path.

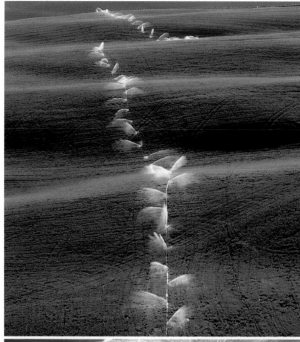

top: *An irrigation system creates a necklace of life, bringing water to an arid area. The water droplets fly like fireworks, transforming the surface.*

above: *Many aquatic animals are superbly adapted to their environment. A dolphin glides through water with the ease of a bird flying through the air.*

above: *The earlier a child is introduced to water, the less likely he or she is to become afraid of the element.*

left: *People live, work, travel and trade on the water. Not only does the economic well-being of these fishermen depend on water, but it is also a means of transporting all types of produce.*

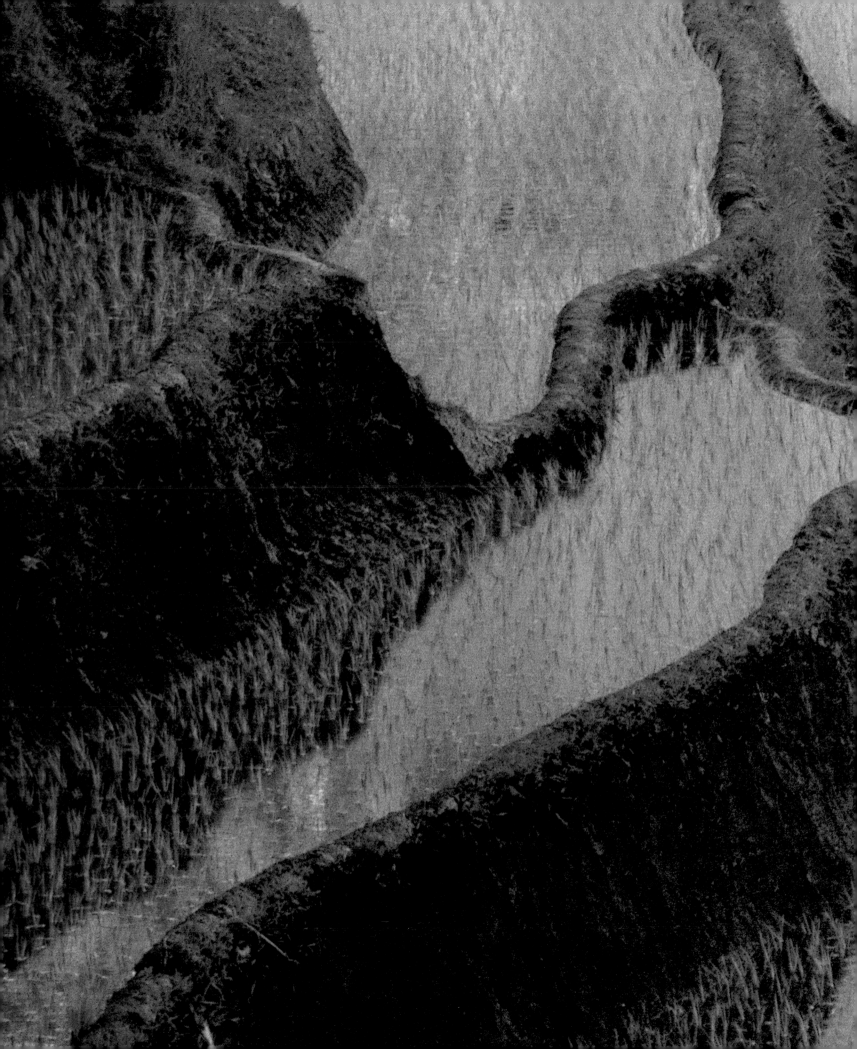

People have always respected the power of water, recognizing the element's strength and potential to destroy or create, and out of that respect grew a great reverence. Water was worshipped and bestowed with deities, from Nun in ancient Egypt, the personification of the primeval waters from which the universe was created, to the beautiful Naiads of Greece and Rome. In Russia, graceful water nymphs called Rusalki were liberated from streams and lakes to sing and dance in snowy meadows during the twelve days of Christmas. The elusive Bunyip haunts antipodean waters, and Urashima, in Japanese mythology, married a beautiful mermaid and lived for centuries under water.

For the Egyptians, water was as indispensable to any paradisial happiness as it was essential to life on earth: the formal water gardens in their ancient tomb paintings represent the perfect homes and gardens of the hereafter and transport the viewer into the sunlit world of Paradise. In one ancient tomb painting a boat glides through the lotus, water lilies and clumps of papyrus. The water teems with fish and the air is full of birds. Nebamon, eternally young, is hunting in the marshes with his favourite hunting cat. His daughter clutches one of his legs to steady herself while plucking a lotus blossom with her other hand, and his wife stands beside him bedecked with lotus. He is surrounded by all that he loves in an environment upon which he could not improve.

Meanwhile, central and western Europe had been peopled by a diversity of tribal communities since before the Bronze Age. These 'Keltoi' or Celts shared a highly evolved artistic and oral literary tradition. Their intense spiritual beliefs led them to dedicate artefacts, votive offerings, requests and even curse tablets to such healing or harming deities as the goddess Sul. Archaeologists have since discovered all manner of dedicatory offerings in springs, wells, rivers, lakes and bogs. The Celts had an instinctive appreciation of the vital links between human life, water and the earth – it is quite likely that modern dowsers employ the same sensitivity to water as these ancient tribesmen exhibited. To this day the names of their water goddesses survive in many of our river names: the Seine was named after Sequana, the Marne after Matrona and the Severn after Sabrina.

above: *The therapeutic benefits of bathing have been appreciated for thousands of years. Baths situated close to the source enjoy naturally heated spring water.*
previous page: *Thanks to the feats of terracing with water in these rice fields, every piece of ground is productive.*

The destructive power of water is a common theme too in mythologies and religions, reminding mankind of his frailty in the face of water's elemental power. Floods in particular are a frequent feature: Jewish and Christian children are told the story of Noah; the ancient West Asian *Epic of Gilgamesh,* cites Utanapishtim as the hero of the flood; whereas Sumerian legends name Atrahasis as the ark builder. Some of the ancient water deities embody this negative force and have more sinister attributes. Many European lakes, rivers and streams are deemed to be haunted by lovely but treacherous sirens – like the one who sits on the Lorelei, a precipitous rock on the River Rhine, luring

sailors to their deaths. Indeed, when I visited the north of Scotland recently I encountered a local superstition dating back to pagan times, which required one human life to be sacrificed each year to the River Spey.

On the whole, however, mythologies and superstitions affirm the beneficent qualities of water. Witches, goblins and demons are unable to cross it, and the notorious witch trials of the Middle Ages often depended entirely on the assumption that water, in its purity, refused to accept the alleged witch's corrupt flesh when she was flung into it. The purifying qualities of water have long played a central role in the ritual of many religions, such as Christian baptism, where the recipient is completely immersed in water or just sprinkled with it.

above: *The nature of a stream can change within a few hours from a trickle to a raging torrent. Excessive storm water may overflow from the stream bed and flood the adjoining fields.*

The enjoyment of water

Our earliest ancestors were quick to realize water's potential for fun and we have exploited this ever since. Evidence of the pleasures of water are to be found in the frescos in the Etruscan Tomb of the Augurs at Tarquinia (*c.* 530 BC), and archaeologists have discovered baths among the remains of many ancient civilizations – in Babylon, Egypt, Europe and South America. The baths at Maen-de-Daro are believed to be about 4,500 years old. Being able to swim was considered a status symbol in ancient Greece, while all classes of Romans revelled in swimming and bathing. For those who could not afford a private bath, great and sophisticated public baths were built. Those at Caracalla, constructed in ad 200, accommodated as many as 1,600 bathers. By around 20 bc the baths had become social gathering places, and aristocratic ladies in Rome would entertain a guest while spending hours on end in the bath clad only in their jewellery!

On the other side of the world, in northern Japan, it was not uncommon for whole families to spend days basking in the hot baths. In the natural hot pools Macaque monkeys immerse themselves as snow falls thickly around their heads. They sit for long periods in the hot water until they are forced by hunger to leave it and plunge once again into the freezing snow. In a delightful woodcut by Hokusai (1760–1849) we see smiling pilgrims enjoying a natural bath at the Roben waterfall in Sagami Province. Turkish and Nordic peoples are also known for their steam baths and saunas, man-made environments that reproduce these natural wonders.

We bathe in water, swim in it, float and sail on it, and play with it. Even a garden hosepipe can offer children hours of fun. When water is frozen we venture onto it to take advantage of the new recreational possibilities it has to offer. Snow entices entire families outside to build snowmen, pelt each other with snowballs, toboggan and ski. Multi-million-pound industries have grown up to exploit water as a medium for sport and recreation.

An increasing awareness of water's link to healthy living – a healthy mind in a healthy body – is improving our lives. Many women today advocate giving birth in water, not only because it is effective as a drug-free form of pain relief for labour, but also in order to minimize the trauma of long labour and birth for their offspring. Dieticians and doctors alike advise people to drink litres of water each day, and physiotherapists extol the virtues of aquaerobics as being the safest and most effective form of exercise for the widest range of people.

above: Hot water from beneath the ground provides enough power for most of Iceland's electrical requirements with plenty left over for bathing.

right: Young people find water jets irresistible. If the nozzles are concealed in paving children can run about safely, darting in and out of the spray.

below: The thrill and excitement of the flume rides are a must at any modern water park.

above: Sea, sails and sky. The water and wind are the media not only for trade and travel, but also for fun and sport out on the open sea.

below: Single jets combine together to form a three-dimensional shape in water, a curving tunnel through which to swim.

left: *Horses and water are often linked in folklore. Scottish myths relate encounters with the sinister Kelpies or Nykurs which haunted freshwater and sea lochs, often changing their shape and carrying off sheep, cattle or occasionally people. Breaking waves are often called 'white horses' and indicate rough weather at sea.*

below: *The artist portrays the idea of unknown terrors lurking in the unfathomable depths of the sea. The fragility of the small craft brings to mind the Breton fisherman's prayer, 'Dear God, be good to me; the sea is so wide and my boat is so small'.*

Water in art

Man's relationship with Nature and the interpretation of her moods is both an inspiration and challenge to artists, writers and musicians. In medieval Europe the Church was the greatest patron of the arts and we find enchanting glimpses of gardens amid predominantly religious subject matter. One such is the small panel painted by the Master of the Paradise Garden *c.*1420 (Staedel Institute, Frankfurt-am-Main). The Virgin is surrounded by attendants in a walled garden crammed with flowers and fruiting trees. While one brightly robed lady offers her musical instrument for the Christ child to play with, another dips a ladle into a stone water trough while a tiny songbird looks on unafraid. In Renaissance paintings tantalizing glimpses of lakes and river appear in the backgrounds of grave and tender Madonnas, such as Raphael's *Madonna of the Goldfinch* of 1506.

In the fifteenth century the Van Eyck brothers included fountains in their devotional pictures, symbolizing the water of life. In these exquisitely detailed works plant forms and landscape were depicted with reverence and astonishing virtuosity: the *Adoration of the Lamb* on the Ghent altarpiece, completed 1432, and the *Madonna of the Fountain* (1439) for example. As artists found more freedom in the attitudes of the religious leaders, they felt more confident to indulge their predilection for landscape and very often waterscape painting.

It is to Protestant Holland and England that we must eventually turn for pure landscape painting. Gradually water, mountains and forests became acceptable motifs in their own right, independent of historical or religious connotations. I have always loved the lively winter scenes by Pieter Breughel the Elder (1525–1569) and Hendrick Avercamp (1585–1634) where peasants revel on frozen lakes beneath atmospheric winter skies – a perfect illustration of water's recreational side.

John Constable (1776–1837) depicted the tumbling clouds, wind-tossed cornfields and limpid waters with the reverence and passionate zeal previously accorded to religious subjects. Earlier, Claude Lorraine (*Pastoral Landscape* 1645) and Nicholas Poussin (1594–1665) had painted the idealized landscapes of classical mythology and in them had placed the nymphs and goddesses of ancient Greece and Rome. It was these painted landscapes that so inspired the great English landscape architects of the eighteenth century. In Constable's pictures, however, ordinary mortals rather than classical deities appear to be completely at home in the sparkling country scenes he depicted. At a recent exhibition, to my joy, I was delighted to discover a French Impressionist painter whose shimmering water paintings I had never previously seen: Gustave Caillebotte (1840–1894) was an enthusiastic sailor and yacht designer, and

he painted radiant waterscapes full of light and colour, and gardens opulent with bright herbaceous borders and vegetable plots of every conceivable shade of green.

In two paintings by nineteenth-century artists, *Hylas and the Nymphs* (1896) by J.W. Waterhouse and *Ophelia* (1851) by John Everett Millais, we see water plants faithfully depicted. The nymphs, skilfully delineated through the clear water, are surrounded by water lilies and a lake fringed with yellow flag iris and water forget-me-nots. Ophelia drifts, decidedly uncorpselike, through a veritable water garden. It is interesting to note that contemporary French painters Renoir and Monet were painting their sensual pictures of nubile girls and water lilies at about the same time, but in a completely unabashed manner and without needing pretensions to any historical or literary reference.

Water is as great a source of inspiration to musicians and authors as it is to painters. No composer has portrayed the excitement of turbulent weather better than Rossini in the *William Tell* overture, which powerfully evokes the charged heaviness of the approaching storm, the thunder's exhilarating crash and the rainwashed calm as birds recommence their song. Schubert's 'Trout Quintet' reflects a quieter mood, evoking the limpid depths below a rippling surface. Johann Strauss was inspired by the steady calming rain at Bad Ischl in Austria: 'A perfect holiday... always rain, the sound of the brook, and a well-heated room where I can write music.' Debussy strove to give musical expression to the sea in 'La Mer', a powerful and brooding piece.

In literature too we have strong proof of water's power to have an impact on the atmosphere of an environment. As far back as the eighth-century saga *Beowulf*, the sinister mere is described as an appropriate home for the monster Grendel and his dam. Later, in the fifteenth century, Chaucer paints a very different picture, giving us an insight into our ancestors' sensual delight in their water gardens.

A garden saw I ful of blosmy bowes

Upon a river in a grene mede,

There as ther swetnesse evermorey - now is

With floures white, blewe, yelwe, and rede,

And colde welle - stremes no thyng dede.

That swommen ful of smale fisches lighte,

With fynnes rede and scales silver-brighte.

More recently, Tennyson, in 'Crossing the Bar', used the flowing of a river as an allegory for the river of life so that the point where river meets the sea signifies his death. The bar is usually choppy, yet he hopes his death will be a peaceful affair, a gentle wave that moves unnoticed from one life to the next.

Water in the garden

Gardens reflect the fact that mankind has always endeavoured to tame nature; the degree of formality varies according to geographical, cultural and historical differences. The Ancient Egyptians built beautiful formal pools richly planted with lotus; the Romans adorned their cities and gardens with pools and fountains. Playful water tricks and pipes hooted and whistled. The opulence and extravagance of some of these led to the downfall of the emperor Nero, whose excessive spending on fountains and water features contributed to the citizens' rebellion. As early as the first Chinese dynasty, which ended *c*.2500 bc, not only the Chinese emperors but also noblemen and rich merchants fell under the spell of water, creating lavish water gardens to resemble natural lakes and mountains.

Seized by water mania, the French kings, just as the Chinese and Romans had done before them, squandered the nation's wealth on outrageously lavish projects like the immense water features at Versailles. In England, vast areas of the countryside were re-shaped by landscape architects like Capability Brown (1716–1783) and incorporated large stretches of water.

Wonderful gardens were built in and around the palaces in the Middle East, principally in those lands situated between the Tigris and Euphrates. Like the Egyptian and Roman gardens, they were formal and based on the canal. This had originally been the means of conveying water from the mountains or rivers and this functional character resulted in the widespread use of a basic rectilinear shape. Sometimes the canals branched off at right angles, giving rise to the quartered garden so often used in Persia. Situated in desert areas, these gardens were intensely sensual, by dint of the contrast they exhibited. Outside lay parching heat and unforgiving rock and sand, inside the sweet tinkling of cooling moving water. Jets played, there were pools for bathing and the scent of citrus blossom and myrtle filled the warm air. The water garden at the Alhambra and Generalife gardens in Granada is a wonderful example of this type of garden. It is astounding how many water features have been used in such small areas: every courtyard, each enclosure, even steps and banisters boast some use of water. The gardens resound to the gentle music of countless jets, rills, dripping basins, water stairs and chutes, creating a delicious melody and a cool, calm and uplifting mood. Particularly amazing are the mechanics, as new water features have been added over the centuries and the whole complex and sophisticated system is gravity-fed.

opposite: *The narrow rill played a vital practical role in conveying water. The small surface area meant that less water was lost by evaporation and the water was easily diverted along intersecting channels by means of a sluice board.*

Until the eighteenth century, Western garden design tended to subject nature to a severe and rigid geometry – directly inherited from the straight lines and rectangles used in early formal gardens from ancient Rome to the Middle East. Even water, naturally so sinuous, was forced to conform to the power of man's controlling logic. For sheer exuberance, nothing can match the gardens constructed during the Renaissance; they surge with a confidence in man's ability to control the natural world. The gardens of the Villa d'Este at Tivoli, near Rome, built between 1550 and 1572, one of the most ambitious gardens of the sixteenth century, continue today to resound with splashing water and the thundering of fountains and cascades. Much in vogue during the Italian Renaissance, *giochi d'acqua* (water effects and tricks) were already being constructed in the time of the Roman empire. Hero of Alexandria had described in his book *Pneumatica* how to engineer elaborate fountains and cunning hydraulic mechanisms such as whistling birds, moving owls and sounding trumpets. In 1580 some of Hero's inventions, many of which were originally designed for the theatre, were employed in the gardens at Tivoli.

The apogee of the European Baroque style is seen in the gardens of Versailles, designed by André Le Nôtre (1613–1700). The gardens at Chatsworth in Derbyshire were originally created in the early seventeenth century by Crelly, a pupil of Le Nôtre, but under the influence of the English Landscape movement the Duke of Devonshire commissioned Capability Brown to remodel the gardens in the 'pastoral' style. As was his style, the renowned landscape gardener removed most of the formal gardens and replaced them with parkland and placid lakes.

At about the same time a very different concept of garden design was attracting attention in Europe, and would have a great bearing on European garden design. In 1749 Père Attiret, a Jesuit priest in Peking, published descriptions of the fantastic 'Garden of Perfect Brightness', the Chinese Emperor's favourite retreat in the 'Forbidden City'. Though constructed by man, the landscapes of this obsessive garden builder imitated nature in a way Père Attiret found quite enchanting. Chinese gardens emulate the streams, lakes and mountains of nature, incorporating water as an essential element. There was no shortage of water and Chinese designers could create large ponds of highly

opposite: Often constructed to glorify a monarch or the church, Baroque gardens became extremely opulent and imposing often incorporating grandiose water parterres.
top: A detail of the intricate workmanship found in Baroque fountains.
above: The Baroque ethos found expression in the dynamic and controlled use of prodigious quantities of water.

convoluted shapes for boating and pleasure: huge rocks were dredged up from the bottom of lakes and erected to represent the mushroom-shaped mountains so typical of China, while streams meandered through valleys planted with plums and willows. Pleasure houses, pavilions and grottoes linked by paths and bridges were scattered throughout the garden and gazebos were placed on bridges overlooking 'the most engaging prospects'. The aim was to create a 'natural and wild view', in sympathy with the Taoist concept of man as a component part of the universal order in nature. Here, indeed, was a very different approach to the strictly geometrical approach of the European Baroque garden designers; this was idealized naturalism that appealed to the senses. Descriptions of these hitherto inaccessible gardens gradually filtered through to the West and reinforced a tentative movement towards naturalism in landscape that was already formulating in England.

Buddhism and Chinese philosophy (with its sensitive affinities to natural landscape) were major factors in the garden art of Japan. In the imposing imperial gardens of Kyoto entire miniature landscapes were constructed. The aim was to create an apparently natural, artless impression, often using borrowed scenery by siting the gardens against a backdrop of impressive distant landscape. The overall impression is less random and complex than the pleasure gardens of China and the effect often more tranquil.

The refined simplicity of such Japanese gardens as the Seinyo-den ceremonial hall (Kyoto Imperial Palace) condenses the Japanese idiom to its very essence. Here water is generally only implied – by raked sand. Often water was placed in simple stone basins, which were used for ritual cleansing, or for bamboo deer-scarers; the regular outpourings and sharp clacking sounds of these spouts were intended to scare deer. The addition of exquisitely grouped stones and the severely restricted planting reinforce an atmosphere reverberating with calm spirituality.

Shrubs are manicured so that they resemble rocks and the pine trees are pruned to give a venerable appearance. Together with simple stone lanterns, they throw their images onto the placid waters and engender an environment ideal for repose and quiet contemplation.

For me, probably the most important person in twentieth-century water gardening was Roberto Burle Marx of Brazil: a genius in landscaping with water and planting in ways which were inspirational to the modern garden design movement. He sculpted the landscape using architectural materials, curving water shapes and mass plantings on a huge scale – as he once put it 'painting the landscape'.

left: *Frank Lloyd Wright's Falling Water is a fusion of modern architecture with a natural fall.*
above: *In gardens inspired by Japanese design principles, the impression of water is often created by other substances.*

source

natural *inspiration*

A spring is the pristine source of water, its rebirth after a long journey underground. Water that emerges from a spring may have moved for hundreds of years through subterranean caverns. Pure and sparkling, it often has curative properties. It is not surprising that we have long revered springs, sanctifying them and dedicating them to deities. A spring may emerge in a pond and the water may run off to form a stream. Or it may be the source of a narrow rill which gradually widens as other sources join it to form a river. Nature uses an almost endless variety of combinations to shape its beauty.

As a child I used to watch as water welled up from the ground in the woods near my school. It was so clear that you could see the parting of the grains of sand beneath the water's surface. Recently I was fascinated to watch the pure fresh water of an ancient spring welling up, freed from its long dark captivity deep underground, sparkling in the sunshine. So glassy smooth, so deep, eternally refilling and emptying, it was like a perpetually shifting mirror.

Springs differ widely in form, mood and strength. Some appear at the head of tiny streams like those I enjoyed at school. Others, such as the Silent Pool in Surrey, England, emerge from the depths of clear pools and lakes, gently swaying the mounds of emerald green starwort that mushroom from the bottom. Then there is the gentle emission of water from a tiny pool filled with watercress,

opposite: The layer of impervious rock on the side of this mountain creates a stunning natural fall as the water makes its way down – a feature that becomes more dramatic after heavy rains.

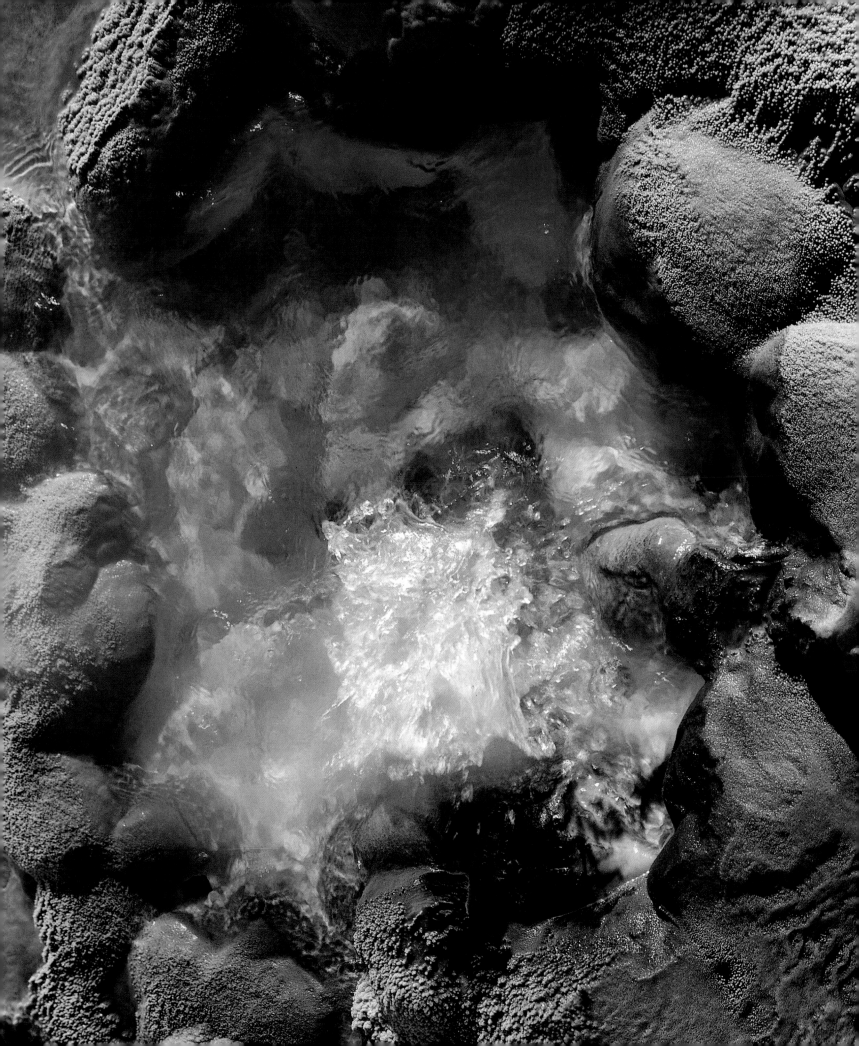

usually found in lower, open, sunny situations. Water may have seeped through hills of chalk to emerge in a clay plane below. Springs in limestone rock often have deposits of carbonate of lime. These completely surround the spring and provide ideal conditions for moss and ferns. They build up into huge mounds from whose depths emerge drips and sprays of water through the glistening greenery.

A patch of sphagnum moss in heathland often indicates a spring, seep or issue. Hidden among the moss you will find water and from its sluggish birthplace in the coll, the flat piece of land where two valleys and two hills meet, it will commence its long descent to the sea.

Still other sources may be traced to caves or small hollows in the rock halfway up or at the foot of hills and mountains. Some emerge from the very bottom of banks and there are springs in France where the water flows from rock tunnels that lead tantalizingly back into the hillside. Some are in caves which are big enough to walk about in. These, partly obscured by a thick canopy of hart's tongue fern, are profoundly mysterious and beckoning, amply repaying the climb necessary to discover them. Each one is different in form and character, with their own particular charms and peculiarities.

opposite: *At Hueravellir in Iceland a geyser surges with hot water from deep underground. Heat-loving organisms paint the surrounding rocks with vivid colour.*
below: *Like islands off a rocky shore, hills and mountains rise above the low cloud. Above the mist the air is warm and dry, whilst below it is very cold with hoar frost covering every branch and twig.*

source features

Any garden, no matter how small, can incorporate a water feature. The different qualities of the source can be recreated even on a tiny scale, from a gentle trickle to an exuberant gush. A patio measuring just 2 x 2m (6 x 6ft) will be sufficient. And there is an infinite range of styles from which to choose. Do you want to construct a source feature which is in keeping with the age and style of your house, or which will look as if it has been there since long before the house was even thought of? Would the complete contrast of a contemporary sculptural fountain be more effective?

below left: *An interesting sheltered water feature whose shape brings to mind an amphitheatre. It is as though the plants are spectators watching the action of the water.*
right: *A striking assortment of wall spouts forms a link between the ornamental pool at the side and the swimming pool itself.*

One way to introduce the life and movement of water into a small garden is with a formal fountain; indeed, in an urban setting, such formality can enhance the surrounding architecture. In a confined space, or by a sitting area, a small fine jet is more desirable than a large vigorous one.

Alternatively, to ensure that the noise of the water does not become oppressive in a small space, you might consider one of the gentler forms of source, rather than taking an enormous geyser as your inspiration. By pumping water through tiny nozzles, it is possible to create a fog garden – a mysterious and exciting world where plants, objects and people constantly dissolve, disappear and reappear. More conventional but just as appealing is the simple bubbling fountain, where water is pumped from an underground tank to bubble or to shoot through rocks or pebbles above, catching the light and making no more than a quiet chuckle.

If you have a garden which incorporates hummocks or steep banks, you might want to recreate a mysterious watery cave. A level garden, on the other hand, is the ideal

far left: *Siting fountains to catch a shaft of sunlight results in a glittering display of water droplets, as well as providing a melodious trickling sound.*
left: *The billowing fog which sprays out from the mist nozzles creates an atmosphere of mystery in à formal open setting.*

location for a more formal design, with a fountain – or series of fountains – which acts as a strong vertical element in an otherwise horizontal design.

Using sympathetic materials in a small garden or courtyard is all-important, because a water feature will obviously appear more dominant there than in a large expansive garden. In an urban setting, you should consider carefully the materials of your own house, and those of the neighbourhood. In a rural landscape, a source feature incorporating natural materials like a pierced millstone or large rock may be appropriate.

Whether you feel drawn towards naturalism or a disciplined geometry, remember that if your garden is to be used by children, safety is paramount. In this case, you should consider installing a self-contained fountain, without a pool, as this is one of the safest source features.

naturalistic springs

If you are trying to recreate a shady woodland spring, it is difficult to improve on nature's example. Secret, unmolested by man and with a long-established natural edge of pebbles and stones covered with moss, ivy and hart's tongue fern, a spring of this type is one of the most beautiful. Rampaging weeds, nettles, brambles and coarse grasses can find no foothold here, so the effect is simple and uncluttered, often with drifts of one species such as snowdrops or bluebells.

This type of spring is easily recreated by means of a small underground tank overlaid with plastic or metal mesh. A small pump in the tank circulates the water. Arrange small rocks, pebbles or old pieces of dressed stone on the mesh, bringing a waterproof lining, either concrete or plastic, up behind the stones. When the stones are backfilled with soil the lining will be completely hidden from view. Drape ivy around the stones, encourage moss to creep over them, and plant ferns into the rocky crevices. Use native species and not only will you get relatively quick results, you will also minimize the amount of maintenance required, as the plants will spread rapidly and exclude weeds.

If you want to imitate a natural cave for a spring, you will need to line the base and sides of the structure, before laying a concrete slab to take the rest of the rockwork. Then it is simply a matter of building up the rocks to form an attractive arch or dome, and installing a submersible pump to circulate the water. See blueprint 1, page 56.

far left: *Water enhances the colours of a collection of interesting pebbles.*
left: *Reminiscent of an ancient cairn, a pile of pierced stones can make a pleasing water sculpture.*

informal fountains

There is an ever-increasing range of informal fountains available today that have neither the traditional geometric appearance of formal fountains nor the rustic air of natural springs. From steel sculptures to fibreglass frogs, most of them come with all the necessary equipment, ready to install yourself at no great cost. A terracotta or glass amphora, apparently randomly placed, makes an intriguing feature with water gushing out, bringing to mind the cornucopia (or horn of plenty) of Greek mythology. Another option is to improvise with sculptures or *objets trouvés*, or even to commission an artist or sculptor to create an original work of art. Anything which can be adapted to house the nozzle of a jet can be pressed into service as the outlet for a fountain. Antique taps, modern sculptures, objects in mosaic, shells, pebbles – all can be used in the design and construction of informal fountains.

between them yet still retain the rocks and pebbles. Build square brick piles to support the stone slabs and the structure will be able to carry quite heavy loads.

The millstone feature, where water issues from the centre of a millstone to trickle over the surface, is particularly appropriate for a country garden, considering its agricultural associations. You can scale down the idea for a tiny garden or patio by using a pierced sculpture, a natural rock or pebble instead of a millstone.

A small rock garden incorporating water makes an interesting feature for a corner, in either urban or rural gardens. Water can be directed into a hollow in a large rock from a tipping ceramic pot with a spout. As the hollow fills up, the water overflows and trickles over the surface, which can be covered with mosses and tiny ferns, before falling into a small pool at the base of the rock. The water is then driven back up to the ceramic pot by a small pump.

A similar device is the Japanese deer-scarer or *sozu kakehi*. This fascinating and unusual fountain is ideal for a garden inspired by oriental philosophy. Water pours slowly into a pivoting hollow bamboo stem which, when full, overbalances and spills its contents. The stem then seasaws rapidly upwards to strike another resonant hollow bamboo. The resulting rhythmic 'clock-clocking' sound echoes throughout the garden with a note that, though pleasing to our ears, is supposedly disquieting to deer.

wall-mounted fountains

The inspiration for the highly popular wall fountains of contemporary gardens goes back to ancient times. Their prototypes were natural springs conducted through apertures in walls, which were often embellished with masks, with a bowl or basin built into the wall so that people could wash their hands and faces, and drink the clear, cold spring water without having to stoop down to the ground. The wall mask takes up

opposite: *Copper pipe can be easily bent into delicate curves to produce interesting shapes. This cluster of tiny jets from the ends of fine tubes resembles a sea anemone.*

above: *Occupying no floor space, a self-contained fountain mounted on a wall creates sound and movement and can feature interesting designs or sculpture.*

Bubble fountains are very easy to construct and cheap to install. It will take no more than a couple of days to recreate a small upwelling or spring effect. Plastic or metal mesh is placed over a tank or bucket which is sunk into the ground and overlaid with small stones or pebbles, or even shells or glass beads. A pump, protected in the tank, pushes water through a short hose to emerge among the stones, before it drips back down into the tank beneath to be recycled. See blueprints 2 and 3, pages 56–57.

For a more permanent and impressive effect with larger rocks or sculptures, use concrete blocks to form a hollow chamber below the ground, bridged by strong slabs on top. These slabs should be far enough apart to let water pass

virtually no space and is therefore ideal for those with small gardens, or even for people with no garden at all, as it can be installed on a balcony or even in a conservatory.

Many natural springs have in the past been enhanced by architectural, man-made settings, for example St Non's Well in St David's, Pembrokeshire in Wales, where a graceful arch of natural stone, dating from the sixth century, encloses the spring. You could recreate this equally well either in a country garden or in the more architectural setting of an urban garden, where a more naturalistic feature would be unsuitable. Siting your 'ancient' spring against a boundary wall will give the impression that the water is flowing in from a neighbouring property. Use a clay or lead pipe, or a pagan mask, as the spout and allow the water to pour into a basin, trough or specially constructed tank.

If you are looking for a wall mask, you could either hunt for a weathered antique one or choose from the many reproductions now available: naturalistic, abstract or grotesque, animal or human. Spouts can be made of bamboo, stone or metal, bamboo being most appropriate for a garden with an oriental rather than a Graeco-Roman flavour. Alternatively, you might like to improvise – with antique taps perhaps.

Old stone or lead troughs are ideal receptacles for the water issuing from such wall fountains; large or small, they are sometimes finely carved with figures, animals and plants. It is still possible to buy old troughs from architectural salvage yards or specialists in garden antiques. If you build a trough out of brick or stone, you can turn it to your advantage: make the rim wide enough to sit on, so that you can rest on a drowsy summer afternoon, dipping a hand into the cool water, watching the fish and enjoying the sound of the fountain.

There are three basic ways to install a wall fountain. If the ornamental tank or trough is small, a separate reservoir will be needed, positioned close by, below ground level. If you have access to both sides of the wall, drill one hole through the bottom of the wall and another at the height you want the mask, and feed the pipe through from the reservoir to the back of the wall and then up to the mouth or the outlet. If you have no access to the other side of the wall, you can either 'chase' a channel up the wall and fit the pipework into that, concealing the repointed channel with judicious planting; or you can build a buttress or pilaster in brick or stone against the wall to house the piping.

These latter two methods will probably be the better options in a town garden, although some neighbours will not necessarily object to having a pipe on their side of the wall, particularly if it has been obscured by careful planting. See blueprints 4 and 5, page 58.

formal fountains

Formal fountains come in all shapes and sizes. Generally powered by a concealed pump, most rise up through a cone, nozzle or ornament set in a visible body of water, such as a pond. Most are characterized by a high jet of water. Reproductions of traditional formal fountains are always popular, but contemporary formal styles of fountain in materials such as stainless steel, glass bronze and copper are becoming more widely available.

The spray pattern in a formal fountain is integral to its design, and the fountain's suitability for a particular position can be enhanced by altering this pattern. The many and varied fountain jets at which we marvel are achieved in just a few basic ways. The classic jet comprises a fountain head with one simple hole producing a thin, straight jet of water, which can be directed to surge vertically or arch sideways as required.

In large open spaces, these jets may be immensely high. When deciding on the height of the spout, however, the rule

left: *These jets have a fascinating shape, resembling a multitude of miniature umbrellas. Used singly they will work in a very small receptacle without splashing and produce some of the gentlest sound effects of any fountain.*

of thumb is that the height of the jet should equal the radius of the basin in which it is placed. On a windy site, a lower jet is advisable; it is less likely to be blown out of the basin, thereby draining the water. The pump driving the fountain may be adjusted gradually until the desired flow is achieved.

For a really dramatic effect, you could have several fountains shooting up from a base of stone paving. The nozzles are positioned just below the surface, and the water drains down through slits in the pavement or through a grating. If, on the other hand, you want to create a gentle bubbling effect in a formal pond, place the nozzle just below the surface of the pool, so that the water barely breaks the surface.

As well as the single-hole type there are fountain heads with many smaller holes, which produce a wide range of spray patterns, from a single fleur-de-lis plume to an elaborate multi-tiered spray resembling an inverted chandelier or a wedding cake. The sumptuous fountains at Longwood Gardens, USA, and Buschart in Canada, all make use of this

effect, with constantly changing water patterns creating the impression of an arching and vivacious ballet.

A flat, slot-like nozzle produces a fan effect, while a strong jet released beneath the surface results in a mound of foaming white water. Mobile jets, like a lawn sprinkler, are also available. The Venturi, a central jet with a separate sheath around it, is placed so that the intake is just below the surface of the water. This draws up water mixed with air and produces a thick, glacial white aerated column.

For larger displays, any number of jets can be grouped together. These are often pre-set at precise angles so that simply by adjusting the water supply, a great variety of effects can be realized – with water shooting skywards one moment, plumes arching from rows of needle jets the next, which in turn give way to a vertical jet that soars up through billowing clouds of mist. These displays are mostly orchestrated electronically, with fountains programmed to synchronize with music and lighting, creating spectacular theatrical effects.

left: *While peering into the shimmering funnel of the water cone you may see a rainbow. At the periphery, drops fly out in all directions catching the light.*
below left: *Like a forest of fountains the jets dance on a paved arena. The water drains back to an underground reservoir where the pumps are located.*
right: *A smooth cobblestone surface set in a radial pattern makes an attractive feature even when the water jets are turned off.*

Jumping jets – intermittent jets of water – delight young and old alike: water is fired horizontally or in a curve for perhaps one second and the resulting bead of water seems to be suspended in the air. The nozzles are arranged to shoot like cannons, or out of the mouths of frogs, and the timing can be electronically or manually controlled.

Unless they are to be placed in a body of water or are purpose-built ornaments, most formal fountains require some sort of reservoir or pool. The surrounds may include edging wide enough to sit on, or a culvert or arch. These can be built from brick, rough-dressed stone or square-cut stone (ashlar). New stone or brickwork can be made to appear mellow and aged by applying liquid manure, rice water or liquid fertilizer; milk and water, or yogurt are good alternatives. You can also press moss into the joints or drape it over the tops of stones to add a venerable touch. However, if you want to sit on the edging around a fountain or trough, it is probably better not to 'age' the stone or you will end up with stained clothes.

The choice and positioning of the pump used to drive the jet will depend on the size and setting of the fountain. Until the seventeenth century most fountains were gravity-fed. Water was piped down from a higher source to create the head of water that would operate the jets. The greater the head above the fountain, the more lofty the jet. This method was used well into the twentieth century. Even now, if a natural source is available in a multi-levelled garden it is worth considering, although surface pumps (requiring the construction of a pump house) are the best option if you are planning a complex series of fountains on several different levels. For smaller features, submersible pumps are adaptable and efficient. You can more or less drop them straight into your pond. Moreover, the high-quality pumps available nowadays are so quiet that you hear only the soothing trickle of the water, not the pump.

For a larger formal fountain, it is better to construct a chamber to one side, to hide the pump and allow access for maintenance purposes. See blueprint 6, page 59.

design uses

Whether you are incorporating a naturalistic spring or formal fountain into your garden, it will play an important role in the overall design. When we are out walking, the merest hint of water close by is enough to entice us to seek out its mysterious source. The sound of a bubbling spring or even the mere glimpse of rushes, flag iris, or royal fern is sufficient inducement, for all these plants spell water. Hidden like this, a spring exploits an age-old design principle: revealing only part of a feature stimulates interest and tempts the visitor to explore. The feature is therefore not an end in itself, but part of an integrated design.

opposite: *Clean water wells up from a central mossy rock in the delightfully enclosed spring pool. The slightest murmur of moving water would be sufficient to tempt one into this enclosure.*
right: *A thin classical jet makes a marvellous focal point among dark evergreens.*
overleaf: *Splinters of light catching water from this beautiful fountain perfectly complement the leaf shapes of these tropical plants and humidify the atmosphere.*

A fountain can be used in the same way: the quiet tinkling of cool fountains behind fragrant myrtle hedges in the formal gardens of the Middle East entices the visitor from one intimate courtyard to another. Tall corridors of aromatic evergreens and silvery beads of water bouncing above a thick hedge draw attention to the existence of yet another secret garden. The path to the fountain itself may be serpentine, but you are likely to be as curious as Alice about what you will find when you reach the garden, and as determined as she was to get there. A grotesque mask or animal head peering out from lush fronds of fern or ivy can provide a dramatic effect.

You may want to use a fountain, both musical and light-catching, as a powerful focal point, introducing life and sparkle even into the dullest part of the garden. Placed at the far end of a lawn, it will lead the eye down the garden and point the way to fresh surprises. At the intersection of two pathways, a soaring plume of water is a strong vertical accent which draws the eye to the crossing. Partially screening the pathway beyond with water, it also creates an air of mystery.

A fountain situated in the very middle of a courtyard or lawn will evoke the sense of balance and repose so cherished by Islamic designers, whose geometric virtuosity is reflected in those elegant, symmetrical gardens of the Middle East. Strong vertical elements, such as lofty cypress trees, accentuated the fountains which were often placed centrally in square or circular enclosures. Similar outside 'rooms' can be created by using walls of pleached limes. Cypress, columnar Juniper (*Juniperus communis* 'Hibernica') and Irish yew (*Taxus baccata* 'Fastigiata') are all appropriate candidates for use in these types of garden.

A surrounding colonnade or pergola may be adjusted to either conceal or disclose the fountain. The addition of trellis work and festoons of climbing plants will create a highly intimate retreat. The intersection of two colonnaded walkways or pergolas is the perfect spot for a secluded raised fountain pool amply large to sit beside. It will also be big enough to incorporate a much loftier jet, one whose beckoning, splashing will be heard from afar.

sound effects

Sound is an important consideration when you are deciding what type of fountain to have in your garden. Achieving the right level of water music is enormously beneficial. At once soothing and refreshing, the sound of moving water calms and revitalizes the spirits and cools the emotions. It can also mask unwanted sounds, such as the sound of traffic in town gardens, lawn-mowers, wood chopping or children kicking a football against a wall. However, the sound of water which may be impressive in a large garden can become oppressive in a smaller area. In an enclosed space, such as a city courtyard, a loud sound of bubbling or gushing water is reflected off the walls of the garden or the house and can become intrusive, impinging on concentration and conversation rather than enhancing them. Similarly, noisy splashing in a conservatory or garden room will preclude any normal conversation,

therefore it is best to install a water feature which has a light tinkling, bubbling quality, rather than a gushing one.

If you have a walled garden and you site your fountain centrally, you will always be close enough to the water to benefit from its masking effect, particularly as the walls will reflect the sound on all sides. In the same vein, in the Topkapi Palace in Istanbul, the sultan had a fountain in his bedroom – to hide amorous bedroom conversation from prying ears!

The sound of falling water from a spout or mask will be reflected forwards by a wall. So, if one of your aims is to muffle traffic noise, remember that the higher the wall, the more successful you will be. If the wall is low, the traffic noise will pass over it and compete with the water noise; a high wall will enable you to hear more of the spring and less of the traffic.

There are a number of ways to adjust the volume of sound or change its character to suit the location – or your mood. Water falling from a height straight into a pool creates a strong sound in the middle to lower range; whereas, with a flat stone strategically positioned to break its fall, the tone changes, becoming more high-pitched. Metal or crockery arranged in the trough or basin under the spout produces an even higher-pitched tinkling note, although water falling into a cup will have a deeper, more resonant sound. Moss absorbs almost all the sound of splashing water, so mossy stones are a good choice for an indoor fountain.

below left: *Movement and sound are created by the simplest of water spouts. Features like this are to be found in ancient towns and villages throughout the world, where courtyards and streets are alive with the sound of running water.*

below: *The cooling sound of the fountain presides over this beautiful enclosed pool area. In the afternoon heat its sound would beckon one from adjacent parts of the garden to come and enjoy an invigorating swim. The whole composition with its clean architectural lines produces an oasis of tranquillity.*

combining with other features

above: *Echoing the graceful shapes of the birch this fountain provides a strong unifying element between the pond and adjacent garden. When you look at one the eye is lead to the other. The strategically placed seating allows one to sit and contemplate the juxtaposition of the two elements.*

combining with other features

Springs and fountains may be entirely self-contained or they may be used in combination with various other features, depending on many other factors: space, time, expense, your taste, for example. By its very nature a source is essential to the functioning of some other features, so if you want a small stream or rill in your garden you have no choice but to have a source as well. In this instance it is as necessary as it is ornamental. Similarly, if your heart is set on a tall, impressive jet of water, the most practical way of achieving this is to incorporate it into a pool or lake. The enormous effort and expense of constructing a basin large enough to catch the spray on its return to earth might be better spent on a practical and beautiful feature.

It is quite possible to combine both formal and informal design elements in one scheme and to achieve a harmonious overall effect. I once built a water garden with straight paving around two sides, with the remainder edged by sumptuous naturalistic planting of aquatic and moisture-loving plants. Water, bringing sound and movement to the pond, flowed from a fissure in the side of a large rock surrounded by water iris. Although the rock could have formed a separate feature in its own right, I incorporated it into a semi-formal pond, its curving sides contrasted pleasantly to the angular stone paving.

In a garden designed for children, a fountain could be constructed to rise out of a paved play area. Whether paving or pool, the catchment area surrounding it must be large enough to contain all the droplets so that children can splash and play in complete safety without slipping.

lighting

Judicious lighting can bring a spectacular new dimension to most types of springs, fountains and spouts. I once saw a deep well that was totally covered in tiny emerald-green ferns; activated by the light of the little spotlights fixed in the stone sides, the dormant fern spores had grown into a captivating magic garden. Covered with a circle of plate glass, this indoor well produced a wonderful light in the room and was also a fascinating conversation piece.

It is quite possible to create a very convincing 'well' without having to dig a deep shaft; all you will need is discreet lighting and a little water for reflections. Use unobtrusive lights in matt black lampholders and point them downwards; they will illuminate the feature beautifully without dazzling the onlooker. Grottoes, small caves, culverts and deep rock pools can all be lit effectively in the same way, so your enjoyment of the garden will not be limited to daylight hours. You can also create an atmosphere of mystery and suspense inside caves and grottoes by using green lighting.

Artificial lighting can really enhance millstone features, and it is relatively easy to install. By siting a white light in the hollow centre of the stone where the water wells up, you will create a lovely undulating mass of white light in the top of the millstone. Other lights can be placed further away, directed towards the stones which provide the base for the millstone. These will highlight the falling curtain of water as it cascades down from the millstone's edge, and the potentially dramatic display of mosses and liverworts that quite often colonize the damp masonry supporting the millstone. The process is straightforward and the effects are outstanding.

Wall-mounted fountains can be picked out by putting a spotlight high on a facing wall, or by placing two such spotlights on either side using low-level lighting tucked back into adjacent borders. An uplighter situated behind a rock in the bottom of the stone catchment basin will provide local light for a spout or mask.

As far as fountains are concerned, I would recommend white light in a domestic situation – however much I enjoy the spectacular play of changing coloured lights on large public fountains. It would be difficult to ensure that the colours were in harmony with the surroundings and the effect would be overpowering in an enclosed area. Lighting in still water is prone to algae and needs frequent cleaning, but fountains set in basins can be illuminated by lights placed immediately below the moving column of water. Here, the light will appear to cling to the water right up to the very top.

Make sure that the light bulbs are hidden from view; it is only the effect of the light that you want to see, not the actual fixture itself. You can always hide light fittings in rocks, low shrubs or planters around your water feature. It is also worth remembering that light reflected on still water may dazzle, so it is generally best to restrict your lighting to features with moving water.

opposite: *Lighting water at night creates new mysteries and hidden depths in sources and fountains.*

above: *Lighting emphasizes the contrast between the glistening black surface of the basin and the white water which falls all around like icicles.*

planting

A good rule of thumb to follow when planting around any water feature is that bold clumps of fewer species are far more effective than a cluttered miscellany of many varieties. Remember that droplets splashing on to water lilies will cause the blooms to close up so arrange any fountains accordingly. Choose a background of dark evergreen foliage or dark tree trunks to display the silvery light-catching qualities of water to best advantage. Strategic planting around fountains can partially screen them to create a mysterious atmosphere.

top left: *Simple strong planting without the use of flowers sets off a fountain to excellent effect.*
top right: *The lush planting in this secluded garden is set back to reveal the simplicity of the fountain.*
right: *The tight clipped box hedging forms an integral part of the composition and its simplicity does not conflict with the water jets.*

You could, for example, drape *Clematis armandii* around a large pagan stone face so that it peers out through the canopy foliage. A strong clump of variegated yellow flag iris (*Iris pseudacorus* 'Variegata') or variegated blue iris (*Iris laevigata* 'Variegata') is effective in the trough or basin beneath the spout because the striped foliage will produce a dramatic shape even when the flowers are over. Zebra rush (*Schoenoplectus* 'Zebrinus'), the charming dwarf cat's tail (*Typha minima*) or a cyperus (depending on height and climate) are also good candidates. Meanwhile, the arum lily (*Zantedeschia aethiopica*) with its ethereal white spathes and elegant, shapely leaves makes a fine contrast with masonry.

Remember, though, that planting in basins or troughs containing a fountain or spout can be problematic: water can splash onto big leaves, channelling large quantities of water away from the recirculating system, leaving you with an empty trough or catchment pond in a surprisingly short time.

Springs tend to be diminutive and can easily be swamped by overplanting; a tiny upwelling rock pool could be completely hidden by plants measuring as little as 30cm (12in).

If order to see your source from a distance, use moss and low ground-cover plants. Conversely, by placing a slender plant that suggests water near an insignificant spring, you will draw attention to it without actually screening it from view. *Iris ensata* Variegata with its slender leaves and lovely flat blooms will form neat clumps. The tall cylindrical stems of the white bullrush (*Schoenoplectus lacustris* 'Albescens') or the common bullrush (*Schoenoplectus lacustris*) could be planted in the water. In hotter countries you could use *Thalia dealbata*.

The sense of mystery is increased by screening most of the feature with plants: here it is only the sound of the rushing water which advertises its presence. Use plants such as day lilies (*Hemerocallis*) in cool climates, Agapanthus in more temperate regions and in the sub tropics swamp lilies will produce great clumps of arching foliage.

Some formal fountains look austere without vegetation, but be careful not to overdo it. Using just one type of evergreen plant will often show them off to best advantage, especially one that flowers once a year. Clipped *Elaeagnus* x *ebbingei* or *Pittosporum tobira* are good plants to place near a fountain. If you have children, it may be best to avoid planting around your water feature as they may accidentally trample over cherished plants.

Fountains on or near terraces and patios are likely to be in a sunny open situation requiring planting to suit. It is an opportunity to choose plants that will thrive in a warm sheltered location. These more formal parts of the garden are ideal for fountains framed in hedging. Box, Osmanthus, and lavender are ideal. Lemon trees in large terracotta pots are also attractive, as are columns of climbing plants such as jasmine that scent the area around the fountain.

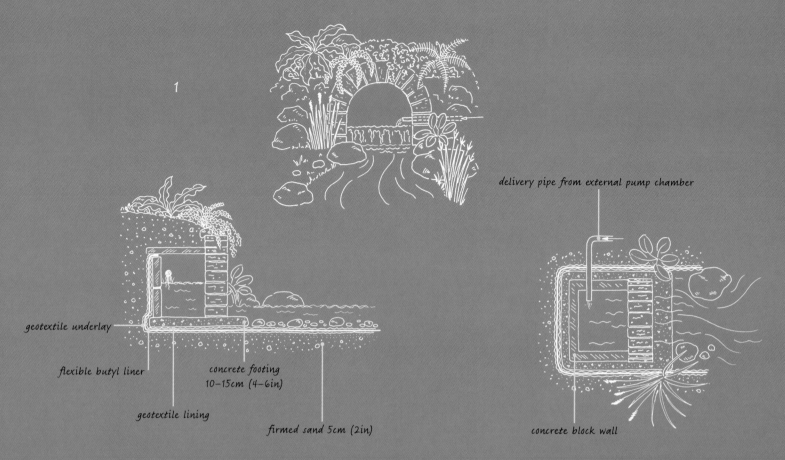

1

delivery pipe from external pump chamber

geotextile underlay

flexible butyl liner

concrete footing
10–15cm (4–6in)

geotextile lining

firmed sand 5cm (2in)

concrete block wall

1 ■ Grotto

A terrace or hillside can be excavated to create a mysterious cave or mossy grotto, partially obscured by lush ferns. The construction method is similar to the bubble fountain but with the reservoir chamber turned on its side. In the illustrated example the excavated chamber has been lined and a concrete block wall built flush against this lining on a concrete footing. The delivery pipe from the recirculating pump, housed in an external chamber, is set in the side of the grotto to issue above the water level. The edge of the liner and geotextile membranes are brought over the top of the chamber walls and mortared in position. Flat rocks or paving slabs form the chamber's roof, or lid. This roof must be strong enough to support the weight of topsoil.

A brick facade is constructed to frame the entrance and across the entrance a low wall forms a lip over which water cascades. Seal the joints of this wall with waterproof grout or expanded polyurethane. Finally the sides and top of the grotto are concealed with soil and planted.

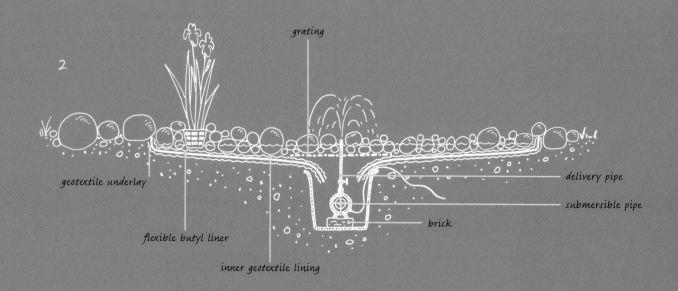

grating

2

geotextile underlay

delivery pipe

submersible pipe

brick

flexible butyl liner

inner geotextile lining

2 ■ Simple bubble fountain

A bubbling spring is one of the simplest sources and for this you need to excavate the surrounding area to about 10cm (4in). In the centre dig a hole slightly wider and deeper than the tank which will form the reservoir. After smoothing the sides of the hole, firm a 5cm (2in) layer of sand over the base. Sink the tank and backfill with sand round the sides, pushing it down firm with a stick. Then line the prepared area with a non-woven geotextile and flexible butyl liner. Cut out a circle of liner and geotextile to expose the tank and lower the pump. Raise the pump on a brick so it is kept above the bottom where dirt will settle.

Then cover the top of the tank with a metal grating or sheet of galvanised mesh, if necessary making a hole for the delivery hose. Arrange pebbles and boulders over the liner mounding them to prevent crushing the delivery hose. It is advisable to test the flow before you complete this stage, as the height of the pump or length of delivery hose may need to be adjusted. Then fill the tank and flood the surrounds, making sure the edge of the liner is pulled up behind the stones. If you wish, water-loving plants can be included in the design.

3 ■ Permanent fountain build like a hypocaust to support a bubble fountain

For a more permanent and impressive fountain build a rigid-sided chamber of concrete slabs and blocks on top of the liner and underlay. The principle of construction is similar to that of the simple bubble fountain but the excavation needs to be deeper to accommodate a concrete foundation necessary to support cement-block walls. At regular intervals construct brick columns to support a roof of concrete slabs. The construction resembles a Roman hypocaust but instead of hot air, water circulates within the chamber. The delivery pipe from the the pump passes through a gap and up, so that it feeds over a piece of sculpture or other outlet mounted on the paving slabs. The slabs may then be disguised with boulders, before the chamber is filled with water.

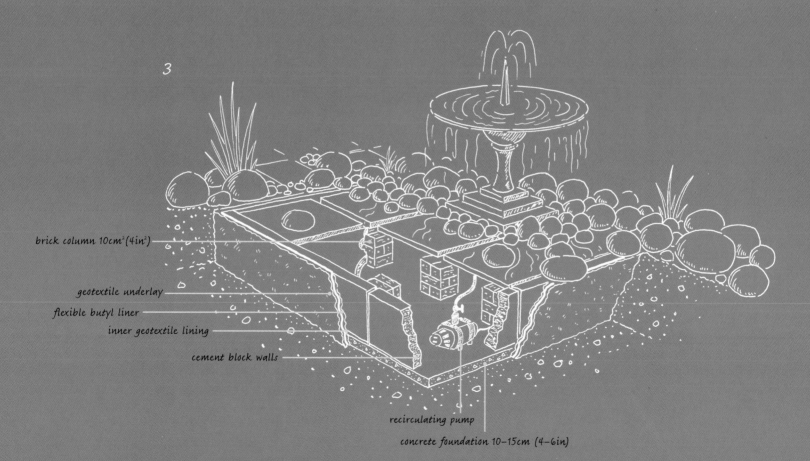

3

brick column 10cm² (4in²)

geotextile underlay

flexible butyl liner

inner geotextile lining

cement block walls

recirculating pump

concrete foundation 10–15cm (4–6in)

Purpose-built reservoir

This is an example of a purpose-built reservoir large enough to house an integral pump chamber. The reservoir is built over a concrete footing which is overlaid with flexible liner sandwiched between non-woven geotextile membranes. A concrete base is spread to support the surrounding walls. The flexible delivery tube runs from the pump to a length of copper pipe which runs up the existing wall. The buttress must be strong enough to support the spout and a thickness of at least 10cm (4in) is recommended. The spout is set into the buttress at the desired height and the delivery pipe fixed with an elbow joint so water issues through an aperture. Butt the facing walls of the reservoir up close to the liners and cover with coping stones. The pump is concealed within a mortared brick chamber topped by a paving slab. This should be left loose for access but can be hidden by marginal plants.

Small reservoir with separate pump chamber

In this example a stone spout issues water into a stone basin, too small to conceal the recirculating pump; so a separate pump chamber in the form of a tank is sunk below ground level to act as a reservoir (as described on pages 56–57). Dig out a hole slightly larger than the tank as described for the bubble fountain (page 56). Once it is in position, lower the pump and join the flexible delivery tube to a length of copper pipe which runs underground and up against the existing wall where it is concealed behind a buttress which supports the spout. Position the stone basin and connect the overflow pipe to the pump chamber.

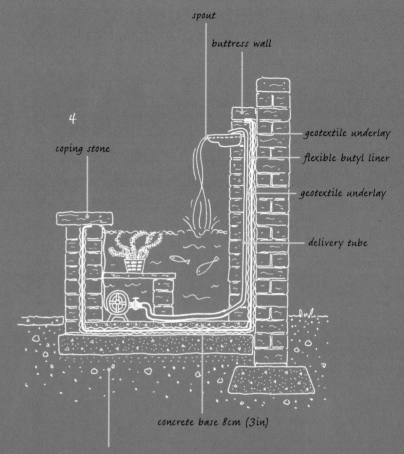

4

spout
buttress wall
coping stone
geotextile underlay
flexible butyl liner
geotextile underlay
delivery tube
concrete base 8cm (3in)
concrete footing 10–15cm (4–6in)

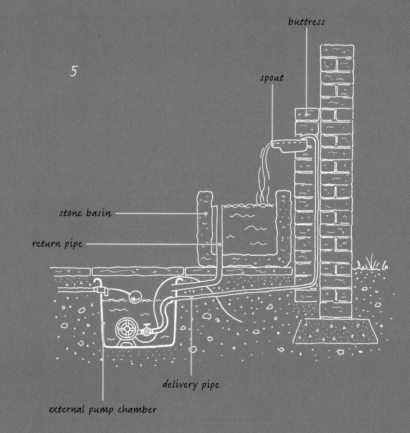

5

buttress
spout
stone basin
return pipe
delivery pipe
external pump chamber

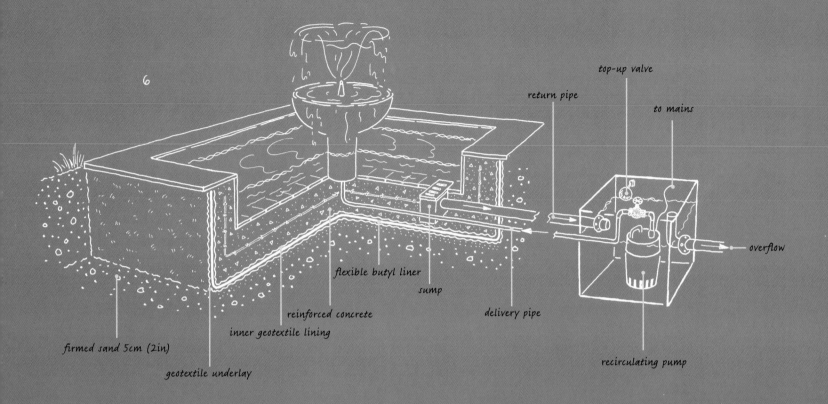

6

top-up valve

return pipe

to mains

flexible butyl liner

sump

reinforced concrete

delivery pipe

overflow

inner geotextile lining

firmed sand 5cm (2in)

geotextile underlay

recirculating pump

6 ■ Formal fountain external pump chamber

For a large formal fountain it is better to construct a separate chamber to house the pump and overflow. This keeps the pond uncluttered and also allows easy access for servicing the pump. The pump chamber can be sited some distance from the water feature which makes its disguise easier.

Build the chamber large enough to accommodate the pump, top-up valve, overflow and a waterproof electrical connection, which must be positioned well above the water level. All electrical installations for any water feature should be carried out by an electrician and fitted with a circuit breaker. Water is pumped to the fountain through the delivery pipe and returns through a duct via the sump. A single paving slab laid over the top of the pumping chamber offers protection and access.

In the illustration the excavation is finished with a layer of firmed sand to give a smooth surface for the layers of geotextile and the liner. As the concrete base is laid, the delivery pipe is run through from the pump chamber and the sump positioned so the grating will be flush with the tiled floor, with its return pipe passing out through the pool wall. Once the concrete base and walls are set they are covered with decorative tiles mortared into position and grouted. The delivery pipe passes up through the fountain within a rigid pipe to the jet fixed at the top.

WARNING: It is most important to employ a qualified electrician to install an outside power supply. The electricity supply must run in armoured cabling in a rigid plastic pipe buried at least 60cm (24in) below ground level, and a residual current device must be fitted to protect the system.

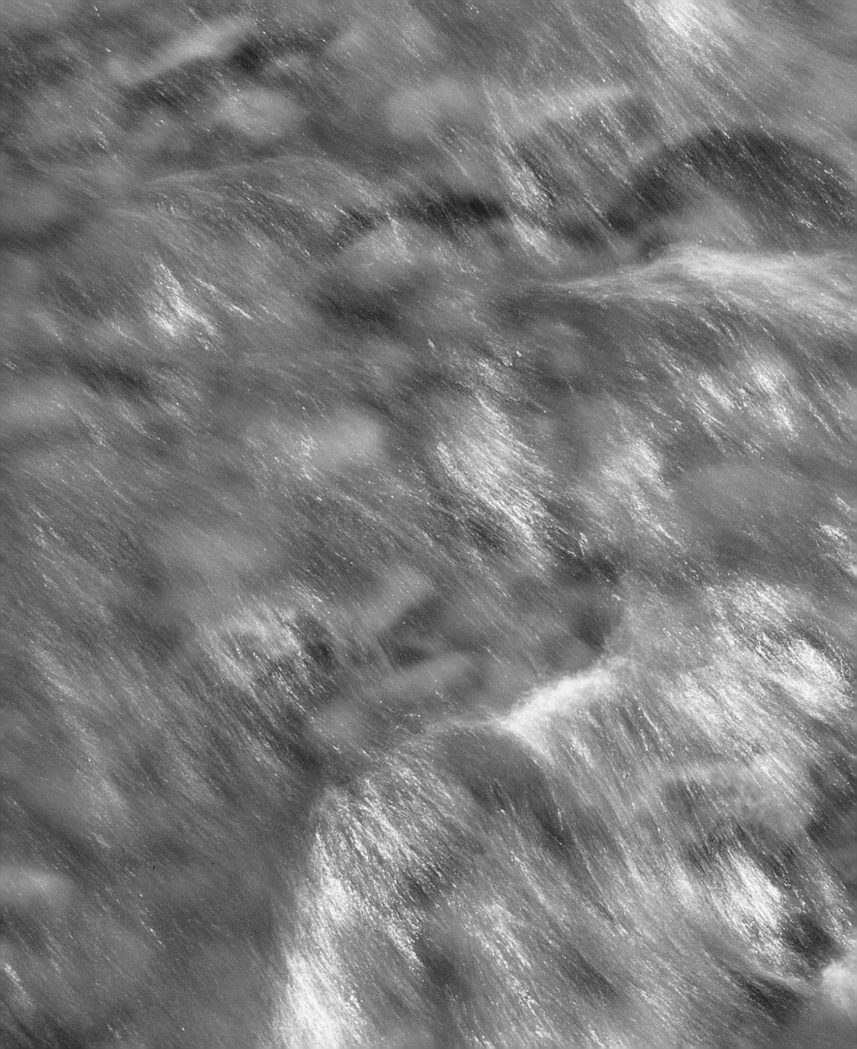

course

Natural *inspiration*

Sometimes rushing and turbulent, sometimes placid and meandering; at times scarcely audible, at others gurgling in deep hollows, rivers are an apposite metaphor for life itself: relentlessly they follow their course to empty themselves at their destination, in a lake or at sea. We speak of our journey from birth to death, with all its twists and turns, successes and failures, as the 'River of Life'. Some may try to go against the flow, others are content to allow life to follow its course and let the current take them.

Rivers are immensely powerful, sculpting the very land itself, carving channels and gorges, creating ridges and carrying rocks and sediment to create new lands. The huge volumes of silt carried and deposited by the Nile in spate transformed hundreds of square miles of arid desert into highly fertile agricultural land and led to the early colonization of this area. Like rivers of ice, glaciers too are capable of sweeping vast rocks along many miles and depositing them in areas geologically quite different from their own places of origin. These rocks, known as erratics, can weigh hundreds of tons.

Long before man domesticated the horse he relied upon water as a means of exploration, trade and conquest. A medley of cultures spread along coasts and rivers as cities grew up, and where no rivers existed men constructed their own in the form of canals. Now these man-made rivers form a complex web of communication, spanning entire continents.

right: An island in miniature, this mossy rock with its tiny sapling replicates larger land masses to perfection. Here plant growth is restricted by the inhospitable surface of the bare rock. Where islands are composed of large areas of soil beware planting vigorous species which may become larger than envisioned and advance across the water's surface.

The character of a stream or river depends on the local geology and topography through which it flows. In gentle rolling grassland water may run over a bed of gravel in the form of a tranquil stream, flanked on either side by thick vegetation growing right down into the water. In summer the bed of the stream is often thickly colonized by such plants as watercress and water forget-me-nots. The stream slides onwards on its way, placid, green and translucent, through arable, pasture and meadows. Without actually peering through the lush vegetation, you can see little evidence of the water beneath it.

The deep shade and heavy leaf fall in a woodland or forest entirely changes the character of a stream. The banks are brown with leafmould, moss clings to the steeper parts, and a splash of bright green where a fern puts forth its fronds highlights the shade. Where the tree canopy is less dense the side of the stream will be clothed in moisture- and shade-loving native species. In northern Europe these would include marsh marigolds or yellow flag iris, wood anemone, and bugle with ivy forming a thick underplanting.

Streams in rocky areas leap and tumble, boiling snowy white, sculpting whirlpools and gullies in the rock, sometimes forming a series of rock-lined pools linked by waterfalls. Plant life is sparse and the beauty lies in the mossy lichen-covered rocks. As the stream runs through heath and moorland its banks might be steeply undercut with great overhangs of heather or turf. Streams and rivers carve the stone in awesome, beautiful, yet logical ways,

below: *The convolutions of a natural river can provide inspiration for a stream or rill through one's own garden. Existing trees and rocks will dictate the route and often demand a sinuous course.*

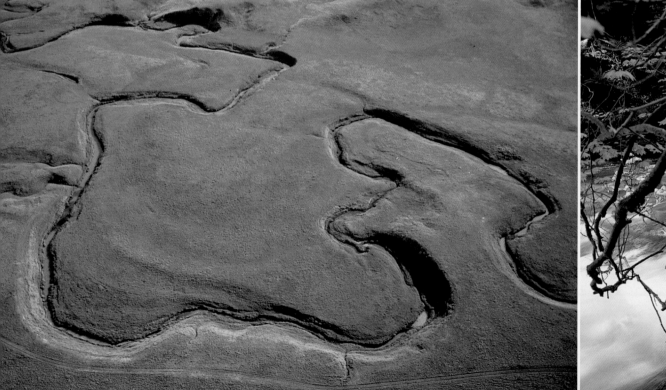

as slowly and inexorably the soft water wears away the hard rock. The streams cut downwards, making their own valleys. They wind steeply down mountainsides, nudged this way and that by the harder outcrops of rock.

A course begins as a spring or streamlet. On the chalk downs of southern England, when the water table rises sufficiently, the water appears on the surface in streams called bourns. A stream may be deceptively feeble at first but, fed by smaller streams, tributaries or feeders, it quickly grows bigger and reaches the playful stage, leaping through the rocks and pebbles. Soon it is strong enough to lift the stones from the stream bed and hurl them or carry them along together with silts, leaves and branches. As it reaches maturity the river becomes wide and powerful. It can carry heavy loads and drive great water wheels. During periods of torrential rain its force is awesome: trees may be torn up by the roots, crops and houses swept away. Towards the end of its course the river becomes broader and much slower. It puts down its heavy burdens of stone, silt and mud, content to meander wherever the contours of the land dictate. It winds around its own deposits, sometimes leaving a part of itself behind – the oxbow lake. The water on the outside of a bend runs swiftly but on the inside it is sluggish. The outside gradually cuts a new path forwards while the inside silts up completely. As the river draws near to the sea, it begins to succumb to the ebb and flow of the tide, as though surrendering to a greater power. The point where the river and sea meet, the bar, is shallow and brackish.

below centre: *The banks of woodland streams often consist of moss, rock and leafmould with low ground cover plants. The simplicity of this edging beneath the canopy highlights subtle water qualities.*

below: *Mountain or coastal streams are often devoid of any vegetation. The complexities of the water movement and intricacies of the rock grain and lichen come to the fore.*

course features

Studying different types of streams in nature will provide insights into what type of course might suit your own garden. If your garden already has a water course, either natural or constructed, this will have a significant bearing on the design of your course. Is the source natural-looking, bosky or stony, or is it man-made with dressed stone or brick surrounds? Is it modern and contrived with pebbles and a millstone, or does it flow from a wall mask or stone trough? Decide whether you want to retain the style of the original source or change it completely, transforming a naturalistic source into a formal one or vice versa.

right: *A rill or stream with a series of falls of differing visual and musical qualities will invite closer inspection and call for a lingering walk along its margins. (Designed by Anthea Gibson and Anthony Archer-Wills)*

opposite: *Brightly coloured fish are restful to watch as they cruise in the clear water of an ornamental pool.*

previous page: *A bend in the stream, a bridge or even a fallen tree add mystery and interest to a water course by partly obscuring what lies beyond.*

A natural stream or spring can look in keeping with any style or period of architecture because it will be perceived as though it existed before the actual building was constructed. It is unlikely, however, that a traditional formal garden with rills and canals would have been created were it not to enhance the geometrical lines of a great house.

Rills and small canals add decorative interest to large formal gardens and tiny courtyards alike. They can also work in informal country gardens. Although their function may be primarily practical – mill leats, stream carriers, pond by-pass channels and canals are features often associated with rural life – the workings of features such as these lend them a fascination, and time and flora can transform them into objects of tranquil beauty. A straight water course could easily issue from beneath a brick arch or wooden bridge and flow on past the house to arrive at a pool.

In nature water is often a common factor linking many diverse features in the landscape, particularly in complex systems with a number of subsidiary channels or pools.

Similarly, water can be used to provide a link between the different styles within a garden, for it is the one element that is equally at home in each. Water flowing close to the house and out across the garden makes a strong visual link between two very different localities. Think about a country house with an authentic source close by, perhaps disguised by an arched springhead or a wall mask: the water might proceed in a formal canal, passing initially between flagstones, topiaried trees and knot gardens, and then flow out into the wild garden beyond. The eye will be drawn in both ways: back to the house and outwards to its destination. This link can be reinforced stylistically by keeping the stream, canal or rill edging constant. A pebble edge started on a terrace could be in complete harmony with the style of the house, and you could continue this as the stream moves away from the buildings and out into dry gravel beds beyond, through swathes of scented shrubs and curving lawns.

above: *A modern application of an ancient theme. The arching jets in this formal canal are designed to create maximum visual effect with minimal loss of the water.*

right: *Instead of causeways dividing areas ot water, canals segregate patches of dry land. By adding waterways to land or islands to water it is possible to create a water maze or archipelago.*

naturalistic streams

Before painting a nude, an artist needs to have a good understanding of bone structure. Similarly, in order to create an accurate reproduction of a natural stream it is essential to understand its underlying geology.

From the source, which may be the tiniest trickle or a mire of peat and grass, the stream begins to take shape as a definite water course. At this stage the geological formations become apparent, although they are sometimes insignificant, where thick deposits may have masked the underlying rock structure. Quite often among the silt large boulders are exposed, and around these beautiful mossy rocks the water winds sinuously. In some places it will spurt energetically, forced between large boulders; in others it will part to pass on either side. A cluster of smaller stones might create a small waterfall or rapid. In streams like this the flow passes over pebbles and boulders, its broken water sparkling brightly. Eddies form behind larger stones and drifts of sand and gravel are deposited as the stream makes its way down the hillside. In an area abounding in rounded stone this is a good type of stream to emulate.

In some streams the underlying bedrock forms the dominant feature and where the water flows diagonally across it a wonderful complexity of water movement is created. Broken pieces of rock lodged at precarious angles result in a range of water patterns, from fans and converging shutes to whirlpools, plumes and aerial fans. A fan occurs where the water runs at speed over a flattish rock whose downstream edge is above the general water level. The resulting fan or plume of water may take on many diverse and wonderful shapes, and when it flies well clear of the stream bed to catch the sunlight, can be described as an aerial fan. This effect is easily replicated by lodging suitable pieces of rock and large stones in the water course. See blueprint 1, page 94.

If you have a natural source in your garden already, it will probably have created its own course. This may be a lovely stream, needing few improvements. If it is rather insignificant, however, it can be widened in places to form more eye-catching stretches. If it is too quiet, waterfalls will create more sound. In those parts of the garden where a less rugged appearance is more appropriate, a well-manicured lawn could flank a section of the stream.

above: *A small waterfall will create a strong focal point in the course of a stream. Place one near a bridge or crossing point, ideally in view from a patio or near a bedroom window where the soothing water sounds can be heard while you lie in bed at night.*

far left: *The rocks and pebbles in this stream need to be set within the waterproof lining.*
left: *Clear shallow water produces beautiful rippling patterns on a stream bed.*

Similar construction methods are used to build all naturalistic streams, whatever the size of the waterway. In most cases this involves using butyl or EPDM liner to construct a waterproof channel. Any rockwork and edging details in the stream itself are then placed within the liner. Obviously the smaller the stream, the quicker, easier and cheaper the finished effect. See blueprints 1,3,4,5,8, pages 94–97.

When constructing a natural stream incorporating rockwork it is important to know your rocks before finalizing the design: you can fix a rudimentary route, but the final width and the shape and number of convolutions will be dictated entirely by the rocks you have chosen. To produce a natural-looking effect, use larger rocks and bury them deeper into the bank. This will necessitate a deeper, wider stream bed with a bigger liner but will look more convincing. Avoid using rocks which are all the same size. Mix large with small and punctuate with planting and drifts of gravel. See blueprint 2, page 95.

Sandstone and schist work well when creating a rocky stream. Complex water courses can be constructed by inclining the rock strata at a dramatic angle, perhaps even vertically. I spent some time building an EPDM-lined stream where the strata are on edge and run roughly north–south. Water slides between fingers and ridges of rock in long, narrow channels. In places these are blocked by fractured pieces of rock, causing the water to leap over into an adjacent trough at right angles to, or even against, the direction of the main current.

The way in which the water enters a stream will have a marked bearing on how convincing it looks. A natural water course will usually start as a trickle, swelling as it is fed by fresh rivulets and springs. In an artificial stream, to increase the flow as the stream progresses you can 'tee' off several hoses near the pump and feed them into the water course at injection points. Thus while one pipe will satisfy the initial water requirement, the next pipe can augment the flow at an appropriate point further down – perhaps beneath a rock, or in a mound of loose stones – and so on until all the water sources have combined, forming quite a powerful current. These injection points can be regulated individually by using gate valves, so that the resulting increase in water as you proceed along the stream will be most realistic.

Gentle meadow streams are not jagged and rocky but have soft banks with vegetation running right down to the water. When trying to recreate a natural meadow stream, I like to follow nature as closely as possible. Along the margins, take the soil down to the water, covering any hard edging or liner that might otherwise be visible. See blueprint 6, page 96.

Rapid streams with dramatic changes in elevation need secure bank retainment. A rock or boulder edging is needed, and you can make this rockwork dominant or unobtrusive. For a dramatic, rocky scheme, use large stones – ideally moss- and lichen-encrusted. For small beaches or planting areas on or just above the high-water mark, a rock or pebble enclosure would support the beach and prevent the soil being washed away, without spoiling the natural effect.

An occasional contrasting boulder will add variety and interest to the stream margin – a mossy boulder among the more angular rocks, for instance. You can also add textural variety by creating drifts of sand, gravel, and shingle of graded sizes. Pour into the water a mixture of river gravel and sand ranging in diameter from 1.5cm (1⁄2 in) down to dust and the current will sort it for you, leaving natural sand and gravel bars along the base and sides of the stream.

In the wild the sides of the stream may not always manage to contain its flow: blockages or sudden spates may cause the river to overflow for a while. You should bear this in mind and when you are placing your rocks, set the ledges back into the land in places, as though the water had exposed them in times of flood and then receded. Where you have boulders, allow some of them to protrude from the drier ground a little way back from the streamside; a uniform line of rock along the margins of a stream could look most unnatural, resembling a contrived wall of masonry.

opposite: A simple, if rather precarious looking rustic bridge crosses a stream reinforcing the effect of a wild natural course.
above: The roar of water rushing over rounded boulders draws people to the foaming white pools. A combination of bedrock and loose boulders produces a variety of water shapes and lends authenticity to a stream.
overleaf: A smooth carpet of moss, or low ground cover plants, accentuates the course of of a small rill. Its very existence might be obscured by choosing long grass or taller ground cover.

formal waterways

Formal waterways – rills or small canals – tend to look best in the grounds of a formal garden, whether traditional or contemporary. Obviously, it helps to make the style of the water course sympathetic to the style of the house. Connecting a formal garden to a house is easier with a formal rill than trying to construct the more unpredictable movement of a natural stream. The very fact that canals and rills are man-made creates a greater opportunity to build something in keeping with a house that is already standing. You could, for example, use the same building materials for the water course as for the house. Beneath their stone capping the canals and pools can have brick walls in paviours or hard engineering bricks chosen to match the colour of the house bricks. The similarity will give the impression that the water course, if not the rest of the garden, was built at the same time as the house.

Equally, in a modern house, one characterized by stone and glass for instance, water of a new and refreshing style may be incorporated. Canal-like pools beside a walkway, with mirrors of smooth water constantly brimming over into a trough, may extend far into a wild garden, maintaining the rectilinear atmosphere and echoing the vast expanses of glass that characterize the house. The water becomes an extension of the architecture, imposing itself upon the landscape just as the seventeenth-century gardens did when their straight avenues and grass rides pushed out into the countryside.

In a large garden with formal and informal areas, the same water course can run through the plot, taking on the different styles as it does so. For example, a natural stream might run through a wildflower meadow or woodland areas, then turn into a rill as it enters a formal lawn or terrace.

An interesting variation on the design of rills, and one that can be adapted in scale to suit the size of any garden, is to incorporate wider sections, resembling pools, along its length. Be sure of the proportions before you begin construction – there is always the danger of ruining the calm classicism of a rill by introducing too large or too many pools. Mark it out clearly and observe the effect from the bedroom windows or from a similar high vantage point.

On a sloping site formal rills offer great scope for a diversity of materials and effects. Stone carved in different ways creates a variety of waterfall effects; bricks set in dentate or diamond courses will vary the texture and alter the musical timbre of the water. The classical Mughal gardens of India exploit these techniques to excellent effect. You could also use tiles to send the water shooting out from a weir in sparkling spurts.

Take your time when starting to construct a rill – if you skimp on the laying-out stage you could end up with a meandering water course or one that is off-centre. Use fine line attached to pegs to mark out the course before construction. See blueprint 5, page 96.

Ground movement and icy conditions impose an enormous stress on a long, rigid structure, making it prone to breaking

below: *Resembling the swirling patterns used in Bronze Age turf mazes, this circuitous rill is based on a design in the Forbidden City, the garden of the Chinese Emperor, upon which were floated cups of wine offered as prizes to party guests who recited poetry. The shape strongly resembles the cross section of a Nuphar blossom.*

in the middle, so do not be tempted to use a simple concrete construction. The rill may be built from reinforced concrete or a flexible liner. Both will ensure the necessary waterproofing and may be given attractive hard facing materials and edgings. Brick or concrete blocks are ideal for forming the walls or facings, being relatively inexpensive and simple to lay.

The edging of formal rills and canals should be precise, crisp and firm as the effect will be ruined by marshy wavering banks. The original construction must be able to stand the test of time. To achieve this, build the edge in stone, brick, steel or concrete. A stone or brick edge is effective in all manner of settings; it has a dignified classical feel to it, and you can increase the overall coherence of a garden design by extending its use to other areas – a walkway, terrace or patio for instance. See blueprints 7 and 8, page 97.

If you want the lawn to grow right up to the edge of the canal, you will need to finish the top of the canal wall with as narrow a hard edge as possible: the wider the masonry, the greater the risk of the grass which covers it dying in hot weather. Sometimes a steel strip set in concrete is used – a very effective method, but one that is quite difficult to build – or narrow, dressed stone tapering towards the top, with the bevel being on the side of the lawn. Alternatively, perforated engineering bricks can be infilled at the top with soil, allowing the grass to root down far enough to obtain moisture from the water. If concrete blocks are used, the 23cm (9in) hollows will also allow the grass to root close to the water. Sprayed or poured reinforced concrete should be finished with a bevel on top like the dressed stone edging. All concrete should be rendered or dyed black so that it is inconspicuous.

above: *Stylistic conformity with modern architecture may lead to a stark, hard-edged appearance. This may be softened by judicious planting.*

design uses

A ny water course running through the garden must either complement or blend in with the surrounding landscape as well as functioning well mechanically. A natural water course will not look right if it is forced to run alongside a ridge or high spot. A valley, however slight it may be, is the place for a natural stream. If no valley exists in your garden, a judicious regrading of the contours may be necessary to create one. Remember that the excavation of a stream can generate considerable quantities of soil so it is often possible to create a convincing valley simply by repositioning some of the excavated material.

right: *Though conforming to the strict geometry essential to a formal layout, the lavender, clipped herbs, citrus trees and the jasmine trained around a hoop transform this rill into a sensuous perfumed garden.*

Avoid cutting into the rootballs of any existing trees. Instead, allow the stream to curve gently around the edges of the canopies. Let logic dictate the sweeps and bends rather than making an arbitrary course. A carefully placed boulder, for example, will provide a good optical reason for the stream to change direction. Rocks protruding like solid ledges below the surface, cunningly arranged to resemble bedrock, can also be used to divert the stream. See blueprint 9, page 97.

creating a focal point

When designing a winding water course, focal points such as statues, specimen trees and dramatic rocks aligned with the longer reaches can be used to lead the eye away and along the stream. Conversely, the stream can be instrumental in drawing the eye to an important focal point. Such devices add impact to an approach or the view from a window, or can be used to mark something such as the end of a lawn.

When viewed along its length a long reach of water may be dramatically foreshortened so it appears to be a mere pool. This foreshortening effect applies even to more formal rills. To help you visualize this, mark out the course of the stream or rill with tapes pegged out on the ground and stand in your primary vantage point. The best length and direction of the water course will become clear, and you can then make any adjustments before you start excavating.

Viewed from the side a stream will appear much narrower than it is in reality. Long grass or high banks will render it invisible. The only indication of the stream's presence will be tall marginal plants and protruding streamside boulders. It may be necessary to adjust the length and the width of a watercourse to counteract some of the distorting effects of perspective. These same effects can be manipulated to create strong visual forms. For example, by creating an elongated canal, it is possible to create the illusion of a circular pool.

A narrow body of water such as a rill may appear clearly when seen from one point but, viewed obliquely, may disappear completely from view. Even when set in closely mown grass or stone flagging, the water of a rill may be totally invisible when viewed from the side. Rather like a ha-ha, it will be something you come across as a complete surprise. [See blueprints 7 and 8, page 97.

journey, interest and mystery

Tennyson in his *Lady of Shalott* describes the river running down to Camelot as 'the road that runs forever'. A river might encounter many surprises on its journey and what lies behind the next bend is a mystery. Creating this constant sense of anticipation is a skill at which the designers of the classical Japanese gardens were particularly adept. Sometimes they used a sinuous stream bed, thickly planted with *Iris ensata,* or a mock stream of raked sand. These might lead past hidden areas, exciting the curiosity of visitors to explore further.

A well-designed water course will exploit this curiosity and provide surprises for the return as well as the outward journey. A stream could lead you on a path around the garden and through many moods, styles and individual delights, whether you are working in the biggest, most unfriendly city or in a tiny country garden. Perhaps we are led through a bright, sunny, open expanse and then into dappled shade among birch trees: this will mark a major change in feeling. Within the broad plan smaller details provide their own surprises.

The stream may unexpectedly widen out into a sunlit pool where fish bask beneath the lily pads. Maybe it disappears behind a bush, only to reveal, around the bend, an expanse of water iris. As the eye is drawn along the bright strip of water a piece of sculpture might become a focal point. If you choose to follow the water in order to examine this work of art more closely, you might be confronted by a fresh surprise as you are led on towards a summerhouse. In fact, I once helped someone construct a stream system that originated in their summerhouse. The source rose up in a circular well in the middle of the building and flowed out through a narrow channel through the floor and on into a shallow stony stream where small flowers adorned the banks. The stream wound round beneath a high bank and flowed into a large circular reflective pool. Here the stream formed a tangible link between the interior of the summerhouse and the garden outside.

On one occasion I followed a tiny rill which ran through a larch forest. However, it wasn't the rill itself which drew me onwards enthralled, but the self-seeded candelabra primulas. Brilliantly flourishing amongst the sphagnum moss the flowers formed a wide, twisting red carpet through the green forest. I was spellbound by their sheer numbers as fresh expanses appeared behind every hummock and bend in the glade.

The tantalizing sound of hidden water splashing at the heart of a maze is an inducement to strive even harder to reach the centre. Such hidden water features recall the Middle Eastern gardens, with tinkling fountains which play in courtyards surrounded by tall fragrant evergreens.

opposite: *One feels compelled to follow this sinuous ribbon of water. It provides a powerful link between different localities and who knows where it leads?*

sound effects

Consider carefully the element of sound when you are designing a water course for your garden. Poets through the ages have striven to evoke the deliciously refreshing sound of a stream: the murmuring and gurgling, plopping and babbling, the smooth rushing and chuckling that sounds as if it is gabbling away to itself. Trying to describe the sounds made by running water is as difficult as describing a colour, perfume, or a sensation, the task is almost impossible. Personally, I find the sound of water simultaneously invigorating and soothing. Tantalizingly audible even above jubilant spring birdsong, a stream may well be hidden away. After the initial thrill of discovering the sound's source, you are then tempted to dally on the bank, lulled almost to sleep by the soporific effect of the water's hypnotic music.

Sound is important in any garden and, as all the sounds and sensations that accompany water are in equal part pleasant, beguiling and therapeutic, the noise of water should be high on the designer's list of priorities. Moreover, the sound of running water can be a strong focus, so you should exploit it. However, be aware of the fact that too much noise can be intrusive and good planning, as always, is crucial. Ask yourself whether the water will be too far from the terrace to be audible; conversely, whether it might be too close. If it is too loud for comfort, it will fail to intrigue, while a mysterious sound is a powerful lure, always tempting people to investigate its source. A waterfall, rapids or a weir fulfils this function in a garden. Use the strongest, most pleasing sound to the best advantage. If you want people to follow the winding course of a woodland stream, punctuate it with small sound effects at intervals, so that as you leave one sound behind, the next becomes audible, drawing visitors ever onwards in an exciting journey of discovery.

Streams do not have to change levels in order to produce sound. If you increase the stream's velocity by adding rivulets at various points in its course, those little tributaries, entering

from the sides over pebbles or rocks, will produce a variety of sounds, depending on how you arrange the stones. A little experimentation will produce sounds of varying pitch and amplitude. This feature works best with small shallow streams, such as those in very small country gardens or in backyards, in walled town gardens, or close to the sitting area in a larger garden. You should mask each injection point with rocks, or small boulders and pebbles, and then the water will murmur or chuckle out from among these.

There is little conceptual difference between the creation of sound effects for natural, informal or formal water courses. The materials and the way in which they are used may differ but the reasons for producing sound in the park or garden are much the same. They all help to mask traffic or industrial noise. If this is excessive then a much louder water system can be created. Remember, however, that a gentle sound created close by will have a similar or better effect than a loud one in the distance.

I once worked with the garden designer Anthea Gibson on the construction of a pair of parallel rills between pleached lime trees at her beautiful Cotswold home. Situated at regular intervals along the rills, each fall was fashioned to make a differently pitched sound. By using pieces of carved stone originally intended for mullions, transoms or fireplaces we were able to create rills whose pitch ranged from high to low as you walked down the lawns beside them. Moreover, the water shot out in different patterns, catching the light in matched pairs down the rills. Broad flagstones were used for bridges and the rills ended in rectangular formal pools, the whole system recirculated by means of an electric pump.

Water falling into water in front of a hollow chamber of stone or brick will produce a deep, resonant note. A higher tone results when water falls onto stone or brick. Often the most musical notes come from water that is just breaking into large droplets from a solid stream; a body of water that holds together during its fall, on the other hand, will generally make a deeper sound. It is possible to reproduce a fall like this by cutting one or two grooves through which to guide the water as it falls, and keeping the streams relatively concentrated. If the water is spread out too thinly, it breaks up into droplets before hitting the surface and you will lose the constant stream of sound as it falls.

far left: *Stone tanks placed in strategic positions along a water course produce varying tones as the water flows through.*
left: *Like the deer scarers employed in oriental gardens, this charming water wheel is designed to create sound.*
right: *Pieces of stone are arranged to strike the raised wooden slats as the wheel rotates, producing melodious tones like xylophone music.*

combining with other features

In nature a stream will encounter rapids and waterfalls when descending a steep slope. These are the 'predictables'. It is likely also to contain rock pools, but these pools themselves are varied and highly individual. Some may be like cauldrons, scoured out by trapped stones whirled incessantly around by the current. Others may be unexpectedly large, allowing the water to idle and spread, and these play host to a variety of plants and fish. The stream may encounter an area of uncertainty in which it opens out into a bog where there is no apparent water channel. The water seeps slowly through, carrying nourishment to the thick vegetation, and then it gathers itself together to continue the downward journey.

These natural patterns supply us with a great deal of inspiration for our own gardens. A rocky stream can include rock pools of differing shapes, sizes and depths. Vary the way the water enters these: one may open out into a large pool or incorporate a bog garden *en route*. Allow the stream to branch and reunite, running at different levels for a while as it parts for larger rocks or areas of bog planting. Once a small island is created by this method, you could put stepping stones or a bridge to reach it from the bank. Adaptations of any of the apparently infinite variations found in nature could be incorporated handsomely.

A small grotto, brick culvert or emerging underground channel makes an unusual and attractive feature in a stream system. Designed to emerge against one boundary of a garden, the water will disappear at a lower elevation on the other. See source blueprint 4, page 58. With the water flowing out of the culvert, along a stream, then widening out into a pond close to the lower boundary, we get the impression that water flows right through the property. To further this illusion, allow a small portion of the lower pond to pass through a false boundary fence at the far end of the garden. Even a line of sparsely tied bamboo poles will serve as a mock fence through which to catch a glimpse of the water beyond.

right: *What lies in the deep sepulchral grotto behind this sunlit facade? A direct line of stepping stones draws the curious irresistibly into the beckoning gloom. In this unusual and interesting feature the stepping stones follow the course rather than cross it, thus transforming the canal bed itself into a pathway.*

In formal gardens where rills or canals take the place of naturalistic streams, there is ample scope for all kinds of exciting and imaginative effects. The narrow rill can be widened as it flows downhill, or it may open out into a reflective formal pool and re-form as a ribbon of water. Islands or stepping stones can be placed in the wider pool, or a fountain can play on the surface. Long, rectangular pools are an ideal situation for a row of slender classical jets – either down the centre or arching from either side to form a tunnel of water down the middle. This latter arrangement is ideal where a central planting of water lilies is envisaged as droplets falling on the blooms cause them to close their petals. Elegant Islamic pools can be incorporated: circular, octagonal, rectangular or hexagonal, or combinations of these shapes, are easy to include in a rill or canal system and they create stunning effects. Animal statues which squirt water, overspilling stone bowls, ponds which brim over into bigger ponds in a shimmer of movement and light are all eminently suitable. Here, too, the water could originate from a grotto.

You can apply the same principle equally effectively to water issuing from a wall mask and pouring into a stone sink, which in turn overflows into a narrow stone-lined rill. It is this rill that leads the water through the garden, punctuated by small waterfalls when the ground level falls away and the water level needs to drop. Ultimately, it could flow into a fine rectangular formal pool at the opposite end of the garden. If you want to give the wall mask greater emphasis, consider substituting a wide gape with a sill for the simple open mouth, the water then falling more generously at the beginning of your feature. Taking this a step further, the emerging water could be made to fall in a curtain about a metre or so in width. These water curtains give a strictly formal impression with overtones of artificiality and architectural construction. They work well, therefore, as separate units, needing no additional streams or rills. Fountains and the more elaborate wall mask features also have an inherent man-made quality ideal in gardens of artifice.

bridges and stepping stones

Bridges are a constant delight for young children, making it possible to reach inaccessible, mysterious, secret places, like islands. Crossing the bridge is an intrepid adventure, but once safely on the other side there is a feeling of security, achievement and inviolable privacy, as if nothing can reach you to interfere. The urge to discover what is on the other side is so strong an emotion that it does not fade even with maturity. We will always be drawn to cross over the bridge and explore what lies beyond it.

A bridge also opens up whole new vistas and enables you to see water plants that you would otherwise never see. The additional height afforded by an arched bridge will give you scope to survey even more of the water course. The sight of a bridge in the distance will suggest that there is water there, and it is a sufficiently interesting feature to tempt a visitor to move towards it through the garden. An arched bridge can be used either to block or frame a view of the stream from certain angles, an important consideration when you are designing vistas from the house, patio or lawn. While it is neither logical nor feasible to span a stretch of water at its widest point, other

factors besides the logical crossing point should play a part in dictating where to site your bridge. You should also consider how the bridge and the paths leading to it can actively dictate a specific route around the garden. You can exploit its linking function too, to unify various elements in a garden design.

If you have access to large, flat stone slabs, lay one across the stream to make an enduring bridge that will not obscure any view of the garden. Demolition companies are a good source of paving stones, doorsteps or lintels which you can recycle in your garden, but if you can only find small slabs, or if you need a longer bridge, use a double span of stones, with the ends of the slabs resting on rocks placed in the water. The ancient 'clapper' bridges of Devon are a beautiful example of this style of bridge.

Planks laid across a stream are practical but have a temporary look; they make you want to cross quickly. Boards placed on two main bearers, on the other hand, give the impression of a more permanent, restful bridge, and invite you to stop halfway to enjoy the view. In a woodland setting you might use rustic half-sawn poles, and edge the path leading to the bridge in the same materials.

Long stretches of interconnecting planks are sometimes used to span wide, sluggish streams and bogs. These may be diverted around trees or deep pools to break the line, which might become too dominant or simply monotonous.

It is essential to treat soft wood with a coat of preservative, for a rotten bridge is a dangerous bridge. Also for safety's sake, a handrail is a good idea. Chickenwire stapled over the wood will also prevent the bridge becoming slippery and potentially dangerous in damp or icy weather.

Stepping stones fulfil the same function as a bridge but have an extra dimension – they require a certain daring. You feel even safer and more inaccessible if your pursuer has to pluck up enough courage to cross the stepping stones to reach you! Stepping stones look more natural than a bridge in an informal setting. I once improvised, using millstones as stepping stones to span a large lake. Arranged in a curving, apparently random, path across the water, they made an attractive pattern, whilst echoing the circular motif which could be found in other parts of the garden.

above left: *Lovely rounded, water worn stones such as these need little additional embellishment.*

above: *Stepping stones are effective in moss gardens, bog gardens and herbaceous beds as well as water. The simplicity of the planting accentuates the colours, textures and forms of the stones and bridge.*

planting

Planting a water course fulfils several functions. It increases the stability of the banks and enriches the ecological environment, attracting many fascinating creatures. The plants help to purify and clear the water. A handsome planting scheme will draw the eye and thus also attract attention to a nearby focal point. It is a way of enhancing the area aesthetically with a variety of colour, texture, form and perfume. It is important, however, to achieve a balance with these elements: beware of overplanting, for in fact a riot of colour and texture is all the more striking when contrasted with some quiet areas nearby.

opposite: *One could almost imagine gazing up at the sky through an avenue of conifers as one looks down at this unusually planted stream. An artificially lined stream will have dry ground right up to the edge enabling plants such as Juniper to be grown where they can fan out over the water.*

Careful forethought and planning will make planting easier and, as time goes on, more successful. Even very formal or stony water courses sometimes need to have areas designed for planting, for the occasional shapely plant will relieve and soften the austerity of hard stone edges.

If you are working with only a small body of moving water, your choice of plants will naturally be more limited, but it is possible to be more adventurous with the surrounding areas. Some plants positively thrive by the streamside. They seem to need the extra oxygen provided to the roots by the moving water, and although the plants themselves are situated above the water, their roots reach down to enjoy the movement of the water through the soil. Among these are several varieties of skunk cabbage which flower in the early spring, all with handsome, glossy green leaves and elegant spathes that look almost extra-terrestrial: *Symplocarpus foetidus* has striking spathes blotched purple and green; *Lysichiton americanus* has large lemon yellow coloured spathes; while *L. camtschatcensis* is more stately and pure white. Many of the hardy primulas

thrive by the streamside and are some of the showiest bog plants of all. Make sure that the planting bays are filled with soil to just above the water's surface.

Planting by the streamside is much like planting a lake- or poolside. Although the different zones will be narrower, they still exist. Outside the stream there is the dry land or xeric planting, then in the damp ground you have moisture-loving plants – hydric planting. In the wetter ground and in very shallow water grow the bog, swamp and emergent plants. Dig the plants into the soil just like any other plant, but be very careful to note their moisture requirements. Those preferring drier conditions must not be put into water that is too deep, and vice versa. Also, you must take care with plants like irises that their crowns are not covered by soil, or they will rot. The soil on a streamside benefits from oxygen carried through the soil particles by the water, whereas in small static ponds such bog or marsh planting tends to be in soil which is low in oxygen. Here the bog plants, which are naturally adapted to low oxygen levels, will flourish.

A natural stream gives scope for a large range of plants without risking the overcrowding that might occur in a small pond or a bog garden. There will be a variety of micro-environments along its bends and reaches. These include shallow boggy regions and sunny meadowland as well as shaded woodland and rocky falls, each the perfect home for several different types of plant. I recommend interspersing tall, slender bullrushes with broad clumps of rounded-leafed plants such as the giant kingcup or marsh marigold (*Caltha palustris*). Further on, plant little gems like *Primula rosea* 'Grandiflora' or *Caltha palustris* var. *alba*, both so welcome in the early spring, or try water forget-me-not (*Myosotis*

left: *Dramatic vertical lines are produced by the bamboo and iris leaves in complete contrast to the horizontal stream edge. This planting is further dramatised by the variation in the textures and greens.*
right: *The stream sides play host to a huge variety of plants whose varied foliage shapes and colours provide interest throughout the growing season.*
far right: *Rocks and stones are accentuated by using simple planting. The undulating carpet of helxine* (Soleirolia) *is also more labour saving than bog and moisture-loving plants.*

scorpioides) with its endearing blue flowers – small, shy varieties that are always such fun to encounter as you walk along the water's course.

Overhanging trees which have a heavy leaf fall should be kept to a minimum as they inhibit plant growth. If you are trying to create a woodland stream, consider only shade-tolerant plants for edge planting. Before the leafy canopy appears, several flowering plants may flourish here, but later, when the canopy is established, you will be restricted to plants that thrive in the shade including skunk cabbage, ferns, mosses and low-growing ground cover. If you are to

plant the woodland through which your stream will flow, it is probably sensible to use those species with light leaf canopies like silver birch (*Betula pendula*), although trees such as oak, beech or maple can be used if the canopies are kept high.

When you are planting directly into the stream the main thing to consider is the speed of the current. Only certain species are able to tolerate fast-moving water: whether it be a brandy bottle or yellow pond lily *(Nuphar lutea)*, which is planted in the same way as a water lily, or a submerged aquatic like water crowfoot (*Ranunculus aquatilis*), you should place the plant in a soil pocket which is surrounded by rocks and

stones, and make sure that the soil is protected from the movement of the water. If the stream in which you are working has a plastic liner, you will need to give your soil pockets on the bottom some extra protection – usually a geotextile membrane placed on the liner is the most straightforward solution here, with the stones and soil placed on top of this. With the exception of some bamboos, plant roots will not penetrate a liner, as they search for just two things – nutrients and moisture – and a liner offers neither of these. Remember that all of the rockwork, the soil, sand and gravel must be placed inside the liner.

Some aquatic plants are particularly useful, performing the vital function of holding together the soil on the banks, preventing erosion: practically all the rushes can withstand strong currents, and the umbrella plant (*Darmera peltata*) is particularly good at holding together loose soil on the banks above the waterline.

Finally, you must be aware that plants tend to creep down a bank into the water and some of them, like the yellow flag iris (*Iris pseudacorus*), will form a clump which may extend some way up the bank onto the dry ground. If you want a very neat edge, ensure that the water is comparatively deep:

left: *Where Koi or other fish are to be shown off in crystal clear water, particular attention should be given to rock, gravel, plants and other underwater elements.*

right: *Erroneously referred to as bullrush, the great reed mace spells water for most people. However, beware planting this rampant colonizer in shallow natural ponds.*

30–60cm (12–24in), and that the bank has a rocky edge. Plant in pockets of soil within the stream and above the rocks outside the stream and you will minimize encroachment, given the two markedly different moisture contents involved.

Purists would argue that a formal rill should be devoid of planting. In fact, formal rills will have little room for planting anyway, but you can create beautiful formal effects using just one plant. I have, for example, seen arum lilies (*Zantedeschia*) used right down the centre of a narrow channel in a French garden. Also, whether it was for expediency or aesthetic effect, I have seen pots of agapanthus standing in rills and blooming with alacrity during the hot summer months.

Use elegant lofty plants like bullrushes – either the true bullrush (*Schoenoplectus lacustris*) or the white Japanese variation (*S. lacustris* 'Albescens') – to proclaim the presence of water and provide a strong vertical accent in your garden. Seen from the terrace or patio, it will be sufficiently distinctive above any surrounding lower planting to lure the visitor to the water's edge. In windy areas, a lower and therefore more robust yellow flag iris might be a more suitable candidate. Fresh botanical surprises await by the stream itself: perhaps some interesting aquatic plant in the shallow moving water – water hawthorn (*Aponogeton distachyos*) with its delicious vanilla-like fragrance, for instance.

planting for wildlife

Freshwater environments support a complex and fascinating abundance of living creatures in the wild, because water which has permeated soil and porous rock will be rich in minerals and nutrients and the temperature is more stable in a large body of water than on dry land. A number of factors including depth, temperature fluctuations, chemical composition and speed will then have a bearing on the watery habitat, so that, for example, profoundly deep water will support less vegetation than shallow because of the absence of light. In areas where the rocks are constantly splashed a rich covering of moss, lichen and algae will soon establish itself, and in the garden these possess a huge advantage in requiring no aftercare. Shallow meandering streams or canals meanwhile encourage flourishing colonies of plant life, which in turn support many varieties of insects, birds and animals.

Fast-flowing rocky streams, however, leave few sedimentary deposits and do not therefore encourage much in the way of plant colonization. The shapes and texture of rock, gravel and sand beneath the swift, clear water set the scene for a submerged garden instead. Underwater plants that enjoy moving water can be difficult to establish, so do not be disappointed if your planting comes to a dead end at this

point, or if it takes some time before you find a plant that thrives in this new home. The plants which may finally succeed here are the water crowfoot species (*Ranunculus aquatilis* and *R. fluitans*), autumn starwort (*Callitriche hermaphroditica*) and also willow moss (*Fontinalis antipyretica*), a fascinating underwater plant with deep green fronds which attaches itself to old roots and stones. Plants whose leaves appear above the level of the water, like watercress (*Rorippa nasturtium-aquaticum*) are easier to grow. In the shallows try planting the bright marsh marigold (*Caltha palustris*) with its reliable early crop of yellow spring flowers, or the white version of this plant, for these will happily tolerate some water movement through their dense stalks.

Once the water is running constantly small creatures will colonize the rocks and drifts of detritus. Small molluscs, caddis fly larvae, freshwater shrimps and water beetles will begin to graze the algae and clean up the bed of the stream. Emergent plants like the yellow flag iris and the aromatic sweet flag (*Acorus calamus*) will soon send mats of trailing white roots into the stream flow, and these extract a good deal of nitrogen, phosphates and ammonia from the water. So too do the bacteria which form in the gravel on the stream bed. This all helps to purify and cleanse the water, so a long stream will serve as a good biological filter for a pond.

Brown trout will survive in cold, highly oxygenated natural streams but not in small, artificial garden streams. Fish will not be happy unless they can get down to a depth of at least 45cm (18in) in the water. Golden orfe, meanwhile, are the hardiest and most attractive fish for cold running water in gardens. Not only do they swim in well-choreographed shoals, but because they live on midges and mosquito larvae they spend a lot of time near the surface. Introduce them into the water as fry and they will grow to suit the stream system. Be aware that if you have a pond in your water course into which they can swim, they will most likely spend the majority of their time in that section, which is most beneficial for them during the winter months.

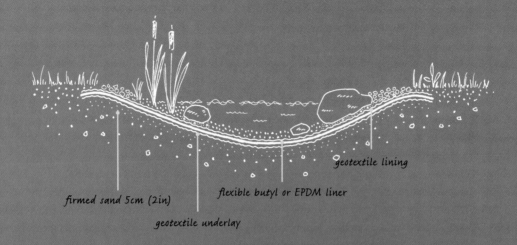

1

firmed sand 5cm (2in)

geotextile underlay

geotextile lining

flexible butyl or EPDM liner

1 ◼ A naturalistic stream

Once you have planned the course of your stream you need to dig a shallow cutting. If you intend to incorporate rocks, the exact depth of the excavation will be dictated by the finished water depth, the height of the rocks and, if necessary, the concrete base. The rocks need to be set well down, in order to imitate a natural cutting or valley, although one or two could stand proud. The width of the excavation will also be determined by the rocks, for they have to be comfortably accommodated, whilst leaving room enough for the water to pass between them. In order to finish up with a stream approximately 45cm (18 in) wide you need to excavate a trough 45cm (18in) plus the width of the streamside rocks. Thus, if the rocks are 1.5m (5ft) wide, the prepared bed will be 0.5 + 1.5 + 1.5m (18in + 5ft + 5ft) plus a little manoeuvring space which means a section 4m (12ft) wide. This seems a vast width to prepare for a narrow stream bed, but your efforts will be well rewarded. In practice, of course, the width of the finished stream will vary along its length according to the profile of the rocks.

In general, streams are dug in sections marked by changes of level or width, so the profile of the excavation will vary according to the character of the stream: where narrow and flanked by grass it can be V-shaped, but if the stream broadens out or large rocks are set on concrete a flat bottom or gently curving profile will be more practical.

Once the excavation is completed and the sides firmed and smoothed, line the trench, working from the lowest level. Set the stones and rocks that form the edging in a bed of concrete or mortar, to cushion the large ones and hold small ones solidly in place. Very large rocks may be set on a sand-gravel mix, packing the void around them with rounded stones. It is essential that the liner comes well up above water level behind the rocks to avoid water loss. Once the rocks – the 'bones' of your design – are in place, you can overlay them with soil and gravel to adjust the planting depths and the width of visible water, mimicking the flow of a natural stream.

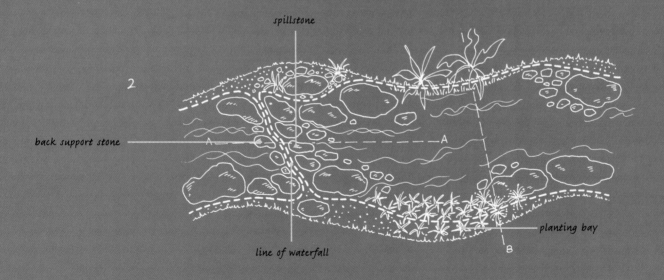

spillstone

2

back support stone

line of waterfall

planting bay

A

A

B

2 ■ Grass margins and planting bays

If the lawn is to grow right up to the edge of the stream a hard edge is necessary. Courses of perforated engineering bricks mortared together and set on a concrete base are infilled with topsoil. By this means the stream edge is supported and grass can grow lush right up to the brink by rooting down into the moist soil within the bricks. Make sure that the liner is folded up to the top of the bricks to avoid water seeping into the body of the lawn.

Planting bays are established in lazy backwaters out of the main flow of the stream. You can establish such areas with a partially submerged meandering wall of small rocks or sandbags. The rocks will not only control to some extent the invasive growth of waterside plants, but they will also retain a deep-water channel in the middle of the stream, which might otherwise fill with silt.

3 & 4 ■ Waterfall and rapids

Small changes of level can be made by shallow waterfalls and rapids made by a partial barrier of rocks. Just before the excavation takes a step down set rocks across the width of the stream to provide back support for the liner. Pleat the liner to match the height of the rocks and mortar it in position. Set the spillstones at the lower level. The spillstones should stretch across the stream and, in places, form narrow fissures where the flow is concentrated. On either side of the spillway position larger rocks of greater height to channel the water over the fall. To prevent water flowing behind the rocks mortar them in position with a waterproof grout and camouflage the cracks with small stones.

Small rocks placed to stand proud of the water further downstream will break up the flow into bubbling rapids, while plants can be established in calm, soil-filled shallows to one side.

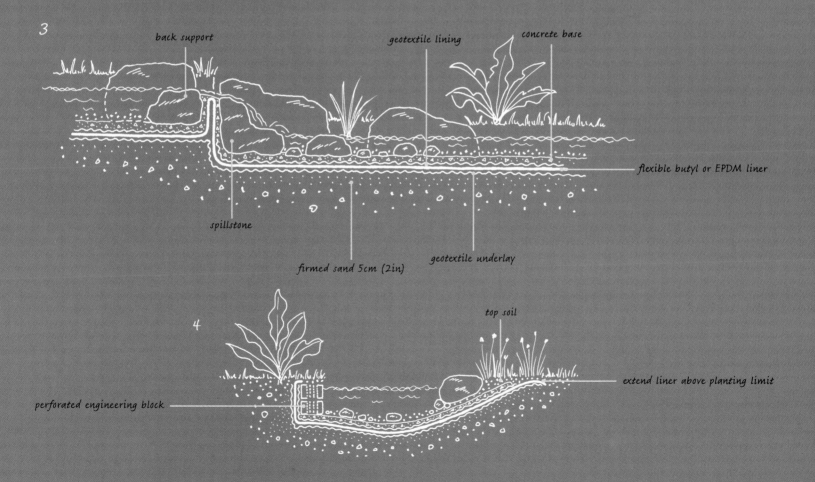

3   back support   geotextile lining   concrete base

flexible butyl or EPDM liner

spillstone

firmed sand 5cm (2in)   geotextile underlay

4   top soil

extend liner above planting limit

perforated engineering block

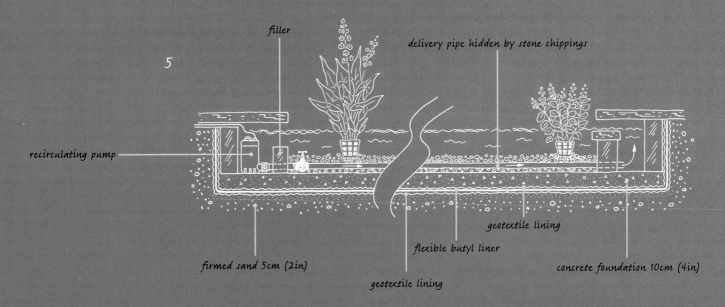

5

filler

delivery pipe hidden by stone chippings

recirculating pump

geotextile lining

flexible butyl liner

firmed sand 5cm (2in)

geotextile lining

concrete foundation 10cm (4in)

5 ■ Construction of a rill

Excavate a channel equal to the width of the finished rill plus at least a brick's width on either side. The depth must take into account concrete foundations. After firming the base, line the channel and lay concrete foundations. Liner alone is insufficient when building formal rills as the earth behind tends to crumble producing unsightly bulges and unsafe edges. The pump and filter are concealed below a ledge at one end of the rill. The delivery pipe discharges into a concealed brick-built chamber at the far end. Strategically placed water plants give additional concealment of the water circulatory system.

For small rills which open into pools of no more than two or three times their width, dig a canal equal to the widest pool. The rill and its pools are then built within the liner, in brick or stonework, on a concrete footing and the 'unused' space backfilled with soil, sand or gravel. If the available space is only about 10m (30ft) in length, the rill should have a width of approximately 30cm (1ft) and could open out into one rectangular pool in the centre and one at the destination.

6 ■ Typical stream course

Water naturally flows downhill so when you first plan a stream look for a natural valley course through your garden. Even if the land is flat the excavation of a stream will generate large quantities of soil. Use the soil to add gentle slopes stretching well back from the waterside. Observe what happens in the wild to design a stream that flows naturally through your landscape. It skirts round tree canopies, and is forced to change direction by a rocky outcrop. Where a change in elevation occurs a natural stream rushes fast through narrow straits or it may tumble over a waterfall then, as it descends more slowly, it broadens out.

6

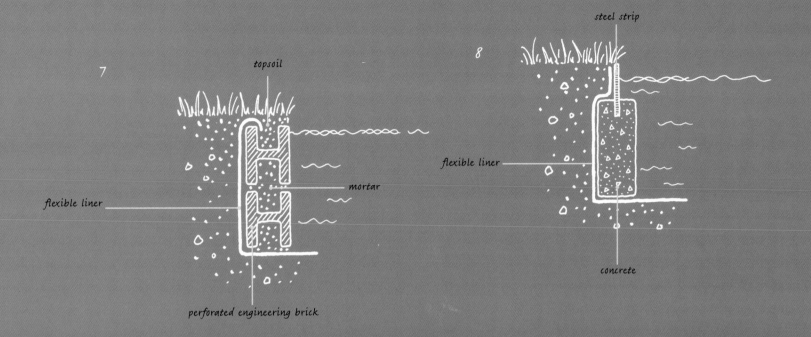

Edging a formal rill

7 & 8 ■ To ensure grass grows right up to the edge of the rill, perforated engineering bricks, or hollow concrete blocks, set in mortar can be used to form the side walls, as described on page 95. It is important to bring the liner well up behind the bricks or blocks. so water can seep down and provide moisture for the grass roots. An alternative method of achieving a crisp lawn edge is to set a thin steel strip in concrete. Take the liner right up the top of the steel and cut it flush to ensure the water is level with the lawn.

Perspective in watercourse design

9 ■ Seen from above it is obvious how the boulders influence the course of the stream and create narrows but, if viewed from the side the water almost disappears and only the rocks and water plants remain visible. When a waterway is viewed along its length it appears as a pool. The effect of perspective is heightened ifthe water narrows in the distance.

WARNING: It is most important to employ a qualified electrician to install an outside power supply. The electricity supply must run in armoured cabling in a rigid plastic pipe buried at least 60cm (24in) below ground level, and a residual current device must be fitted to protect the system.

outlet

natural *inspiration*

Both streams and rivers incorporate an inspiring variety of waterfalls as they make their way downhill, each with its own particular character. These range from the merest chuckle as the water drops a few centimetres over mossy stones, to spectacular and dramatic plunges of several metres. After meandering on its course through meadows, pools and pastures a stream will display a sudden and startling change of mood when it encounters a steeper descent. However lazy the flow may have seemed before, now it leaps and bounces, revitalized, over rocks, as it tumbles down the slope. Multiple waterfalls, where the water descends over a sequence of rocks, may have an open pool between each drop or may be choked with random boulders or pieces of broken ledge. Each individual fall may be little more than 30cm (12in) in height, and yet the water will be wrought into a diversity of shapes as inspirational and fantastic as those in any great cataract.

Although I would go out of my way to walk through a wood to find a stream, I would happily drive for miles to visit a waterfall. While working in the United States I visited the spectacular Kent Falls in Connecticut, on several occasions, despite the hour-long drive it took to reach them. Each time these cataracts were in a different mood. In early March, when they were all but obscured

right: Refined and elegant, the complex movements of the waterfall's vigorous headlong rush are caught by winter's icy grip. The main tendencies within the fall, together with all horizontal or random trends, are clearly defined. We may easily compare the course of the most powerful flow, the more tentative side runnels where the water explores a possible future route and the delicate clusters of icicles where the water constantly splashed. Some people run their waterfalls in winter in order to enjoy the lovely ice scuplture they produce.

by mounds of snow and mammoth icicles, they resembled the soaring majestic pipes of a great cathedral organ, the water appearing only at intervals, in the cauldron-like pools where it swirled deep, translucent and green. In summer the water fell gently from pool to pool. Children plunged in and out of the deeper pools and basked lazily on the surrounding rocks to dry off. After two days of torrential autumn rain the falls were violent, striking the low branches of surrounding trees and shooting out from beneath rocky projections in great clouds of spray as the water ground away at the rock, trying to tear it from its hold. It was a violent manifestation of rock in conflict with water.

The all-embracing term 'waterfall' is entirely inadequate when trying to describe the vast gamut of moods and effects produced by falling water. Natural or formal, the ultimate shapes and patterns of every fall are formed by the objects encountered by the water. The speed and angle of the approaching water will also have a decisive effect upon the water patterns, and on the sounds they make. On a still evening the cool and inviting sound of a waterfall can be heard from afar, and we are incited to explore its individual intricacies, examining the rocks to see how each of the smaller falls which contribute to the grand fall works. The magnificent and enticing qualities of waterfalls should be exploited to the full when choosing a garden feature incorporating falling water.

opposite: Like an emerald green fur mantle, the soft moss envelopes the rocks, protecting them from erosion.
left: A mass of tumbled rocks beneath the surface causes the water to fly off in fan shapes, echoing the leaf forms in the foreground.
centre: Often there is a break in the waterfall where the water has carved out a rock pool.
above: A protruding rock will make the water fly clear of the face in free fall, giving rise to a deep thunderous roar when it hits the pool below.

outlet features

Apart from an occasional formal sheet or curtain of falling water, most waterfalls occur as part of a system. They may be fed by a stream or rill, or they may be the outlet from a pond or lake. The point at which the water enters a pool is the ideal site for a waterfall because there is almost certain to be a reduction in elevation there. All outlets, however, have a pool into which to fall. Natural cataracts scour out their own pools by erosion; artificial falls need an accompanying artificial pool to collect as much of the splashing water as possible. Water falling into a large pool or lake will send out hypnotic ripples across the still water, gently lifting and rocking aquatic plants such as water lilies. In order to create a large expanse of water it is often necessary to cut deeply into the surrounding higher ground, and the drop that this creates may be considerable. A waterfall is the obvious way to link the two levels and will enhance the area.

When choosing an outlet feature to suit your garden, opt for something which is restful and pleasing to the eye. Include an occasional element of surprise, which will give zest to a design. It is perfectly logical to site a natural waterfall by a house of any style or period, because the building might well have been so sited in order to enjoy the close proximity of the water. Frank Lloyd Wright's beautiful 'Falling Water', in the Appalachian foothills, where the water falls right underneath an overhanging wing of the house, is a fine example of integrating a building with a waterfall.

Cascades comprise a series of straight falls built in natural stone, reminiscent of those seen in seventeenth-century Baroque gardens. These were built from squared, closely fitting stone, which was often carved to resemble natural rock.

Cascades are particularly suited to seventeenth-century buildings, but they are equally suitable for gardens of houses built in the style of that period.

As the name implies, a water staircase is a series of regular falls of severely formal design. Some variety may be introduced in the height and width of each step, and the lips might be carved or constructed in different ways to vary the direction or the speed of the flow of the water over them. Water stairs blend equally well into either a town or country setting where the garden is sloping or terraced. Such features are best situated in more formal surroundings. They need not necessarily be on quite the same scale as the famous example at Chatsworth; scaled-down versions of such grand schemes can be equally striking.

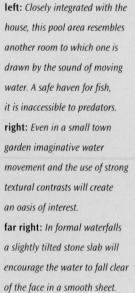

left: *Closely integrated with the house, this pool area resembles another room to which one is drawn by the sound of moving water. A safe haven for fish, it is inaccessible to predators.*
right: *Even in a small town garden imaginative water movement and the use of strong textural contrasts will create an oasis of interest.*
far right: *In formal waterfalls a slightly tilted stone slab will encourage the water to fall clear of the face in a smooth sheet.*

An effective feature for a limited space comprises a single sill over which water pours, creating a close, shimmering curtain effect without any splashing. In a flat garden where no major reconstruction is planned which might bring about a change in level, a water curtain or nappe is one of the few waterfall features which would not look amiss. It consists of a narrow trough built into the top of a wall with a level lip of stone, slate, brick or other smooth material over which the water can pour, and a basin or trough below to catch the falling water. Of a suitable shape and size to sit well in the garden or conservatory, this catchment basin should be large enough to provide a reserve of water for recycling. This type of fall suits a formal garden which calls for a formal device, and is particularly appropriate for modern terraced gardens. It is also possible to construct such a feature on a small scale, and install it indoors.

A series of tinkling falls can be incorporated into even the most slender of rills. These may be built to follow the centre or sides of a staircase. In just this way the Moorish designers took every opportunity to avail themselves of the benefits of cooling water, even conducting it down the handrails beside flights of stairs. Such waterfalls lend a charming 'Arabian Nights' flavour to the garden, evoking as they do those at the Alhambra in Granada, Spain.

If you want to retain stretches of water in a sloping garden you will need weirs or barriers of some kind. Mellowed by age, these gates, originally essential to both canals and watermills, have gathered a romantic charm and appeal over the centuries. Their purpose was temporarily to raise and lower the water level in canal locks or to regulate the flow of water to mill wheels. Now their glistening dark wood, often centuries old, often harbours a garden of water mosses and small aquatic plants which anchor themselves in the crevices.

You can build effective but small wooden weirs quite easily from rot-resistant timbers: discarded railway sleepers are ideal. The water is allowed to flow through a section cut out of the top board. Whether the weir or waterfall is in wood or stone, you must take into account the penetrating scouring action of the water immediately beneath the fall, which could easily undermine the structure. A splash plate constructed below the fall will overcome this problem. Large stones placed under the fall below water level suffice for small weirs or waterfalls, but larger cataracts call for stronger reinforcement. For these, the concrete base on which the waterfall is built should extend out some 2m (6ft) or more to receive the force of the falling water. Make sure that this is well below water level so that it does not show. Disguise the concrete with a covering of rocks and boulders appropriate to the style of the waterfall.

naturalistic waterfalls

For me, building informal waterfalls is the most exacting and rewarding of all water garden construction projects. A naturalistic waterfall is not something which can be precisely decided on paper prior to construction: the concept can be laid out and general instructions given as to the angle of rock strata, types of water effects and flow rates, but each rock is so individual that its actual placement and juxtaposition to other rocks is a matter of artistic judgement rather than one of following a blueprint instruction. Indeed, given the same rocks and the same briefing, five different people will construct five entirely different waterfalls of varying merit according to their skill and personal stylistic choices.

Waterfalls sometimes have a very disordered and jumbled appearance with rocks in seemingly inexplicable positions; this results in a wondrous complexity of water shapes. Making a waterfall look natural means trying to replicate as closely as possible the elements to be found in nature. Try to avoid contrived-looking level sills with a rock on either side to contain the water. Maintain the waterfall within a valley, as though it has been cut by nature, and position some rocks off to the left or right of the composition to avoid symmetry.

above: *It is delightful to be able to sit near moving water, drinking eating al fresco or just thinking. Water clinging to the face of the rocks or taking short plunges is quiet, but the sound can be magnified by increasing the flow.*

right: *The natural stratification found in sedimentary rocks often creates a combination of horizontal and vertical water movements.*

Natural waterfalls occur on exposed rock ledge or chokes of broken rocks and boulders; the rock should appear to rise up out of the water, so be sure to set your rocks below the water elevation. Once a waterproof lining has been established, anything is possible in terms of imaginative rockwork set in concrete or gravel upon the liner. Therefore remember you must always make adequate allowance for protecting the liner.

Decide first of all what is the most suitable type of rock for your particular situation and having selected the best available, turn your attention to the size of your rocks. Choose the largest pieces you can manage and then the rest should be an assortment, the smallest about the size of a fist, useful for 'fine tuning'. Remember that fewer and larger rocks give a greater and more authentic visual impact than heaps of small ones.

The shape of the falls will depend on how the rocks marry together. Height and width can be set precisely but the actual creation of the falls is ultimately in the hands of the builder, although some preconceived effects can be achieved if particular rock shapes are carefully selected and two or three pieces are appropriately juxtaposed.

Practically speaking, you should site waterfalls where the ground falls away most steeply. If, however, this is not feasible in the overall garden design, you can move the fall up- or downstream as required. If you move a waterfall downstream its brink will become higher, relatively, above the sloping ground; to prevent any overflowing and to modify this unnaturalistic effect, you should build up the adjacent banks. It will look more natural if you move the fall back upstream, excavating progressively deeper until the desired point is reached. The further back you cut, the higher and more dramatic the fall will be. Excavate too far back, however, and the the fall will become hidden in a dark gorge and you will then have to cart away large quantities of earth to bring it back to light – unless, as I do, you like these shady mysterious falls with their hidden pathways.

First you must excavate the channel for the strong central flow which runs headlong along the easiest route – the powerful, dark water flowing smoothly along until forced suddenly into fragments by prominent rock formations to produce comet tails of bright droplets pouring down into the pools below. After that you must position the liners and

above left: The dense plant growth and dark background increases the mysterious quality of this waterfall. The sound will be resonant and make a powerful lure to a more hidden part of the garden.

above: Gentle falls over smooth rounded rocks exude tranquillity. The rock pools with their dark reflective water are more inviting to explore with the added interest which the water plants make.

following that the rocks – which you should set in concrete or smooth gravel according to their individual size and situation. See blueprints 1 and 2, pages 124–125.

It is with these rocks that you can create all the complex and intricate water patterns caused by water contending with them: aerial fans that occur when the water pours down a shute to hit a smooth upwardly inclined stone; converging falls that meet in plume-like configurations; swirling back eddies and flows that run contrary to the mainstream; and side sluices that pour off protruding rocks to meet the main flow at a lower level. See blueprints 3,4,5,6,7 and 8, pages 125–126. All these variations will add to the excitement of the fall. If you design natural-looking waterfalls which are then incorporated into long streams you should take your example from nature, ensuring that steeper drops are characterized by more exposed bedrock and a cleaner look. Water may plunge dramatically sheer in this situation, or shoot out clear of the rock face and there will be a dearth of smaller broken rock. Different rocks will suggest new and varied effects to you so the construction work will grow more complex as it progresses.

A permanent gentle flow will encourage mosses and lichens and stimulate the beneficial bacteria in the gravel which help to keep the water clear. This will also be economical to run. However, it is far more interesting to be able to vary the flow rates of a waterfall, each variation bringing fresh details into play. By incorporating a high-flow-rate channel from the beginning, you are constructing another 'natural effect', for you are actually simulating what might occur in nature during a flood that happens once every ten years. The raised water level will overrun different rocks and create new shapes and patterns, and the greater force will generate more spectacular aerial plumes and fans. More air and oxygen will be mixed in with the water so that white broken water will bubble up over the rocks and boulders, the gentle melody of the trickling fall becoming a loud full-throated roar, calculated to impress the most blasé of visitors or to lend excitement to a special occasion. Inevitably, the latter option will result in a greater water loss through evaporation and the surrounding rocks will glisten with moisture, but if you are an avid plant-lover it will also offer far greater scope for you to grow moisture-loving plants. You can adjust the level of the flow in various different ways. You can inject more water through different pipes, or occasionallly – though this is rare because it is expensive – you can use a variable-speed pump.

A natural waterfall's particular character will be defined by the general composition of each aspect of the fall; each will add variety and drama to the water movement. Falls which are angled differently are more interesting than those which follow one another in a straight course. The latter tend to look more formal. Try to create different effects and angles with each fall to maintain the visitor's interest. Straight falls of similar height and width resemble water stairs. It is mainly the water itself which is the focus of attention in this type of cascade; it catches the light in repeated symmetrical falls in a controlled and rhythmic shimmer. If you want to soften a rigid, formal impression, you should use rough, weathered stone and plant heavily on both sides.

You may assume that it will be necessary for you to scale everything – plans and materials – either up or down, according to the scope of your plot. There is far more engineering work in a large waterfall and the heavy rock-work may require a substantial footing or even a sub-base, if the ground is soft. As soon as a rock can no longer be lifted by hand it will require very careful handling by machinery. Small waterfalls should present little problem, but in fact small rocks can be equally as awkward and demanding as large ones, requiring just as much attention to detail and position. Moreover small rock pools and falls will not be secure if the stones are not set in concrete. Any rock that is light enough to be moved by the weight of a person's foot must be considered at best a potential liability, and is also at risk of being moved either by the natural forces of the water or ice or even by an over-zealous weeder.

opposite: Even the tiniest garden waterfall can be made to appear convincingly natural by uncontrived rockwork. For inspiration, study the falls in small streams and brooks in the locality. Many waterfalls of this nature are formed by a choke of broken rocks and pebbles being washed down jamming the watercourse. Small stones and silt get lodged behind making the whole structure waterproof. Such a stream and fall would be easy to construct using a flexible liner.

formal falls

Unlike natural waterfalls, formal falls and cascades are usually reasonably accessible. They are generally set among pathways or terraces, or are surrounded by areas of stone, brick or concrete which may be walked on without damaging the surface. You can often walk right up to the fall and even walk behind the curtain of water on occasion. They can provide the same pleasant sound effects, exhilaration, calm and well-being as a natural waterfall and are just as cooling and refreshing. See blueprint 9, page 127.

Formal falls and cascades often form part of a scheme which links the garden with the house or nearby terraces and pathways. They are generally given more prominence than their natural counterparts. If there is a series of long ramps in the garden, these could be an ideal place to situate a water staircase. A flight of stone steps can be flanked by water on either side. A series of level lawns terraced by stone retaining walls can incorporate brimming geometrically shaped pools linked by water pouring over wide sills from one level to the next. If the topography of the garden allows, the first few pools can be constructed quite close to the house, as the smooth shining sheets of water are restful and unobtrusive. They run more quietly than broken water and almost resemble polished masonry. Any straight, machined, pressed, cast or other man-made architectural materials will cause the water flow to take

on a symmetrical or formal appearance. Formal cascades also work well in woodland settings, in areas of dappled shade where the water will catch the occasional beam of sunlight and sparkle as it falls.

Although formality has overtones of repetition and pattern, it is quite easy to create a more informal, less rigid effect by mixing formal shapes. A water staircase can incorporate spillways of different heights, or one could manipulate the water to leap in different directions and at different speeds and volumes. Conversely, if roughly hewn natural rock is used to construct a waterfall with spillways of uniform height and width, the resulting effect will appear as a time-worn formal symmetrical design rather than as a natural fall. Water stairs can start or finish in a great cascade as the water enters or leaves them from a greater height. It looks more appropriate if the water finishes in a grand fall into a pool or canal, and is more practical too as splashing is avoided.

A system that incorporated the full range of formal falls would be overly complex. However, by using just three differently shaped sills you can create exciting contrasts with shapes, sounds and light effects.

If the falls are positioned to emanate from a source above head-height, perhaps from concrete beams with the water plunging down into fine gratings, children could run in and out of the water, although it would have either to be purified if recirculated or to come from a pure source.

opposite: *Widely varying effects can be achieved by adjusting the flow rates over formal sills and water stairs. Low flows will produce lines of drops whilst high flows create a smooth sheet of water.*

left: *Precise, carefully constructed rims and weirs are vital to achieve this brimming evenly cascading effect.*

above: *A well-engineered sill will throw the water clear in a smooth sheet.*

formal falls **113**

design uses

A waterfall is a dramatic feature and you may want to position it so that it can be seen from the house. The first garden I built was designed along these lines: in the far corner was a high bank, visible from the dining-room window, with fields beyond. A series of linking ponds and sunken pathways generated enough soil to create a valley running down towards the house. From the waterfall the house could be seen peeping through the trees and shrubs at the end of the valley. A smaller path branched off to the left where a glimpse of water iris and a steep bank promised further interest when one had explored the main route.

right: *Water flowing from the mouths of sculptured devisces draws attention to them immediately and in an intimate area, such as a swimming pool, only a gentle trickle will be necessary. If a water feature is designed to attract attention from afar, then the falls must be higher and stronger.*

The tantalizing distant flash of brilliant water will draw the eye up the garden towards the waterfall and invite further exploration. Whether it is designed as a long-distance focal point or a surprise element, the waterfall must blend sympathetically into the surrounding garden. The scene should essentially be restful.

The interest which waterfalls, curtains of smooth water or water stairs bring into a garden cannot be overstated. During a tour of the garden, this is the point where people are almost guaranteed to stop, look and enquire about the origins or workings of the feature and contemplate the changing patterns of light, movement and sound that it creates.

Water stairs are equally beguiling. Seen from a distance they resemble stone steps leading from one part of a garden to another. The foreshortening effect of perspective makes the treads of the stairs appear deceptively short. In fact, the water of each step may stretch back several metres, warranting closer inspection. And if you walk up and down beside a water staircase, you will notice a variety of details that were not visible from further away. Subtle movements in the water caused by irregularities and cracks in the stonework, or moss parting the flow, add interest and arrest the attention.

When planning a waterfall, try to capitalize on the powerful appeal which waterfalls have to all the senses. The glint of light on water is always magical, whether by day or, with clever lighting, by night. Waterfalls are also wonderfully tactile, compelling us to reach out and touch the water as it falls, and providing an instant feeling of refreshment on a hot summer's day. If you have a natural waterfall, the process of clearing sticks that become lodged and watching them go bounding down the falls is also enjoyable. The dynamic textural effect

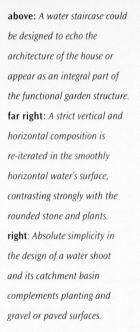

above: *A water staircase could be designed to echo the architecture of the house or appear as an integral part of the functional garden structure.*

far right: *A strict vertical and horizontal composition is re-iterated in the smoothly horizontal water's surface, contrasting strongly with the rounded stone and plants.*

right: *Absolute simplicity in the design of a water shoot and its catchment basin complements planting and gravel or paved surfaces.*

of white water can be contrived deliberately by arranging long runs of broken rocks, jagged rows of bricks or cobble stones.

Shallower slopes may get choked by rock and tumbled boulders, but these in themselves can produce intricate and varied waterfalls where squared and rounded rock, splinters and plates all jostle together to produce a fall of multiple effects. And where a stream levels off below the falls there is likely to be a plethora of rocks and stones carpeting the stream bed, so it is an ideal place for a 'display' of beautiful rock.

sound effects

The first hint of a waterfall's presence is its sound. I once built a waterfall in a garden in the south of France whose purpose was to lure people by its sound alone out of the enclosed garden and into the woodland beyond. The warm Provençal wood was filled with the spicy scent of pine needles, thyme, rosemary and santolina, and bright with cistus and small seasonal wildflowers. Despite this, people tended to congregate in the area immediately around the swimming pool. It needed the sound of a distant waterfall to entice them away. A slight dip running through the steeply terraced contours some 200m (220yd) beyond the garden wall proved to be the ideal position, although the falls needed to be loud to be heard. A tantalizing, steady roar in the distance now draws people from the swimming pool into the fragrant, ever-changing woodland.

As you approach a natural waterfall you gradually become aware that the noise you hear initially is, in fact, a whole symphony of different sounds, rather as white sunlight is composed of all the colours of the spectrum. Each splash, ripple and fall produces sound waves of a different pitch and quality. The range is immense, from the lightest tinkle of droplets hitting stone to the deep resonance of substantial volumes entering the water in an unbroken torrent. A 'sounding box' of hollow rock behind the waterfall will enhance the deeper tones. A well-constructed waterfall should contain notes ranging from treble to bass.

The sound of a waterfall can usually be adjusted after the main construction is completed. You can fine-tune using smaller stones; major chutes of water can be checked and diverted or split up into a number of smaller flows; small trickles can be increased by borrowing water from an adjacent flow. All these adjustments are made by placing stones at strategic points in the water currents.

Changing the flow rate of any large waterfall will also alter the volume of sound quite dramatically, because the varying volumes of falling water will strike different rocks, bringing

new falls into play. It is also a good idea to increase the flow rate further downstream so that the falls increase in power, drama and noise as they run downhill. This will emulate natural falls and appear more authentic.

Formal cascades, sills and falls tend to be less complex in their sound than naturalistic falls, each one producing a distinct note. By grouping the cascades within earshot of each other you can achieve harmonious chords. Whether the fall is formal or naturalistic, the water will fill the garden with that beckoning, soothing music which simultaneously uplifts and calms the spirit and invigorates the senses.

opposite: *An ingenious use of buckets results in a sonorous water feature which is also an amusing conversation piece. The sounds produced can be adjusted by varying the depth of water in the containers.*
above: *A hollow chamber behind the waterfall will increase the resonance and depth of the sound.*

practical uses of waterfalls

As well as being an arresting focal point, a waterfall can have several practical uses. Composed of single or multiple falls near verticle drops, the plunging water will churn oxygen into the pool where it falls. If you have fish, they will love it, basking in the moving water like people in a jacuzzi. Here, too, they find small edible creatures which the falling water stirs up.

Often falls are constructed as part of a filtration system. From a gravel pool above, the water can be made to percolate down into a network of perforated pipes leading to a catchment basin. This overflows as a waterfall into the pond below. The water is recirculated by a pump and the waterfall runs continuously, keeping the pond clear.

Waterfalls and weirs are also important as barriers to form level stretches of water in natural streams. By inserting a series of low barrages in a steep section of stream the flow rate can be reduced from a headlong, highly erosive torrent to a controlled sequence of placid pools and waterfalls. Provided that the banks are high enough to accommodate the falls without the water overflowing onto the surrounding ground, this arrangement has several benefits. Erosion is reduced; the sound of falling water is created; and pools are formed, which will be colonized by plants and animals. Where the waterfall is feeding into a lake or pond, a pool situated behind it will act as a silt trap. It is far easier periodically to remove the accumulation of mud and debris trapped here than it would be to clean the bottom of the larger catchment pool or lake.

lighting

The dramatic impact of cascading water is heightened when one comes upon it suddenly or in unexpected places. At night when illuminated the effect is intensified and the feature takes on a dreamlike quality. By, night the approach to a fall can be precisely determined: subtle lighting can tempt the visitor to

venture into the darkness, to follow a course specifically designed to display the water feature to maximum effect. Steep slopes, steps and sudden curves need to be well lit for safety reasons, for although the route may wind circuitously past scented shrubs and climbers or night-scented stocks (*Matthiola incana*), the path itself should be smooth.

Well-concealed low-level lamps or sparsely-placed mushroom fittings work well to produce appropriately subdued but effective lighting. Alternatively, you can sink uplighters into the ground to illuminate the trees. These are very effective provided they are angled so they do not shine into the eyes. Do make sure, however, that you hide the light source itself. Lamps may be placed to shine downwards from high in the trees but these tend to be rather obvious if one glances up.

When you arrive at the waterfall, it is the tumbling water itself that you should try to highlight. This is not as easy as it sounds, for a direct light tends to shine through the water onto the background, making the water almost invisible. Try placing the lamps to shine obliquely from either side or put them underwater directly beneath the curtain of falling water. An assistant can shout instructions from the best vantage point as you experiment with various positions. As no two situations are ever alike this somewhat hit-and-miss approach works best, for in the end one is assured of achieving the desired effect.

opposite: Waterfalls add oxygen
to the water as they rush down.
left: Lighting the torrent of
a waterfall is effective. Light
is carried up the column from
lamps hidden by the turbulence.
above: Wide weirs will maintain
a very precise water level even
when the flow fluctuates.

pages 118–119:
left: A highly confined fall will
not splash and the sound will
be restricted to a minimum.
centre: A high fall hitting rock
produces a high-pitched sound.
right: Tall steps in water stairs
create a loud note and increase
the oxygen present in the water.

planting

The world's great waterfalls have a unique microclimate, the mist and spray resulting in the creation of localized 'rainforest' areas. A similar effect is created by a garden fall, albeit on a smaller scale. Although the surrounding area is usually well drained because of the steep terrain, the immediate vicinity of the waterfall will be saturated with droplets and mist released by the cataract. Obviously, the higher the fall, the more moist the surrounding atmosphere. A small country-garden waterfall will moisten the air within a few feet creating a humid atmosphere, and the surrounding area will be damp – ideal for moisture-loving plants such as primulas.

There are many varieties available but my personal favourite is the tiny *Primula rosea*. Barely 10cm (4in) high, it carries tight clumps of deep pink flowers that appear before the leaves. It is a good idea to add some contrast by introducing a fern or two: the autumn fern does well in sunnier locations and has delightful finely cut bronze fronds. The more compact forms of mimulus are ideal creeping between the rocks of a sunlit waterfall. Carpets of *Omphalodes cappadocica* with its vivid blue flowers, punctuated by the occasional appearance of a candelabra primula, will make a spectacular scheme. The striking green-and-white stripy leaves of *Iris laevigata* 'Variegata', on the other hand, still provide an interesting foliage contrast when the flowering season has passed. In the slightly drier areas a little way off from the falls the large and often variegated leaves of hostas provide an excellent foil for feathery astilbes and rodgersias, and to these you can add the slender elegant *Iris sibirica*. Even though flowering seasons are ephemeral, there is a great deal of colour and interest to be found in many forms of foliage.

For larger falls in more natural locations such as woodlands and open meadows I prefer to use native plants as they tend to flourish, look more at home and are easier to maintain. Simple planting schemes work best, showing up well from a distance. Some of the loveliest waterfalls I have seen have had a maximum of three species of plant around them. I saw one fall almost smothered in helxine (*Soleirolia soleirolii*), others in one or two species of moss: the simplicity of these planting schemes had a stunning overall effect. The zone and the acidity of the soil will dictate which species to choose. In contrast, planting scheme which is overly fussy can detract from the grandeur of a fine rocky waterfall.

far left: *Ferns are ideal near water, there are all sorts of varieties to suit locations ranging from cold to tropical.*

left: *While some mosses luxuriate in the wet conditions beneath the fall, other plants from above advance as close as they dare.*

Apart from mosses and ferns, wooded areas are often home to just one species of plant. This third native plant adds individuality to the waterfall. I have seen falls embellished in this way by trilliums in Connecticut in the United States, bluebells (Hyacinthoides non-scripta) and the starry white flowers of wild garlic (Allium ursinum) in Sussex, England.

Many artificial cascades and waterfalls lack the high ground behind them that would form the backdrop in a natural setting. This is where background planting is absolutely crucial. It is possible to create the illusion of higher ground by planting shrubs and trees of increasing heights behind the fall. Where the contours of the land are particularly adverse, evergreens will give the required height all the year round: holly (Ilex), Portuguese laurel (Prunus lusitanica), mountain laurel (Kalmia), yew (Taxus), rhododendron, elaeagnus, osmanthus and viburnum are just some of the other good candidates to cultivate in this situation. For more height, you could plant deciduous trees to rise above in the background.

For a more immediate effect in a small garden, the evergreen climbers honeysuckle, (Lonicera japonica 'Halliana') and Clematis armandii look beautiful trained over trellis or domes of wire netting. Thread some ivy (Hedera) through these and you will soon achieve an attractive dense background to the waterfall. Slower growing shrubs can also be planted to take over from the trellis when they mature.

above: *Many plants in the moist conditions, and the brilliant candelabra primulas especially, love the movement of water through their roots.*

opposite: *The tall slender stems of thalias and grasses contrast well with the rounded leaf forms.*

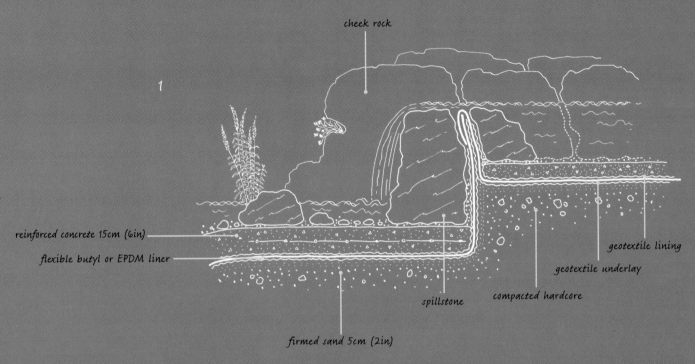

1

cheek rock

reinforced concrete 15cm (6in)

flexible butyl or EPDM liner

spillstone

compacted hardcore

geotextile underlay

geotextile lining

firmed sand 5cm (2in)

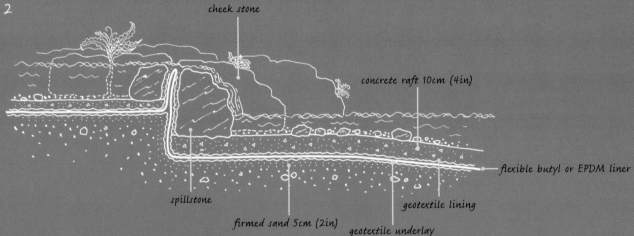

2

cheek stone

concrete raft 10cm (4in)

flexible butyl or EPDM liner

spillstone

geotextile lining

firmed sand 5cm (2in)

geotextile underlay

Large naturalistic waterfall

A sloping site offers the opportunity to create this, the most challenging of garden features. Once you have excavated the channel, smooth and compact the soil, especially round the step of the fall, the edge needs to be very firm. If the ground is at all soft a 10cm (4in) footing of compacted hardcore covered with sand will provide a firm base to support the rocks. Although a water course can be covered with a single length of flexible liner, for a large-scale project it is easier to line each section of the stream separately, starting with the lowest and working uphill. Once the area is lined lay a thick raft of reinforced concrete to provide a firm base for the heavy spillstones and other rocks.

Now position the main spillstones. These must be higher than the ledge. The flow of water can be tested using a hose then, once you are satisfied, the liner and layers of geotextile can be brought up over the ledge and the spillstones concreted in position. On either side of the spillway 'cheek' rocks, which are larger than the spillstones, channel the water over the fall. To prevent water flowing behind the rocks fill gaps and fissures with a waterproof grout or self-expanding polyurethane camouflaged with small pebbles or rock chippings.

The upper pool is constructed in a similar fashion with the liner brought right to the top of the rockwork and folded over by about 30cm (12in), as shown. Smaller rocks are concreted in position behind the spillstones to act as a back support, tightly sandwiching the liners.

2 ■ Small naturalistic waterfall

Small changes of level can be marked by a shallow waterfall constructed in much the same way as the large waterfall opposite. As the rocks are less massive, concrete footings of 10cm (4in) should suffice and a hardcore base prove unnecessary unless the soil is very soft; a 5cm (2in) layer of compacted sand should be adequate to smooth out rough soil. In this example, the back support and spillway rock are set at an angle so the water runs smoothly over the surface, eddying into the lower pool. A single length of liner covers the watercourse and is pleated to match the height of the waterfall rocks. The stream runs smoothly over the concrete footing disguised only by gravel and small stones which the flow will sort.

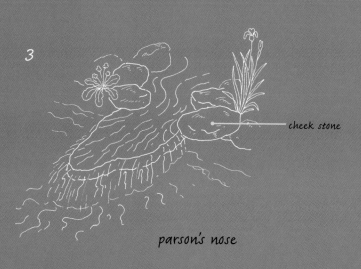

3

cheek stone

parson's nose

4

converging falls

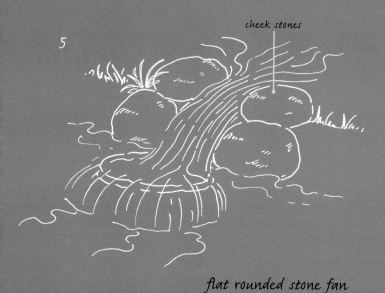

5

cheek stones

flat rounded stone fan

Spillstone styles for naturalistic waterfalls

The shape and positioning of the spillstones greatly influence the mood of the waterfall but, whatever the effect, all rockwork must be concreted firmly in position and grouted, as described in for the large natural waterfall, opposite.

3 ■ The parson's nose is an elongated, fan shape. In this example cheek stones narrow the course so water races over the jutting flat spillstone and flies off around the edges.

4 ■ Converging falls flow through fissures in a semi-circular arrangement of spillstones. The contrast between the smooth upper reaches and the water plummeting down onto bed rocks in the pool below is most exciting.

5 ■ When a fast-flowing stream encounters a flat spillstone with a smooth, round edge the water splays out in a smooth fan of droplets.

6 ▪ By concentrating a broad flow between closely placed cheek stones a plume of water is thrown up resembling a rooster's tail. Make sure the cheek stones are high enough to channel the water.

7 ▪ An exceptionally high vertical fan of water is thrown up when a fast flow hits a flat smooth stone jutting out at a near vertical angle. A fall of only 30cm (12in) is necessary to achieve this lively effect.

8 ▪ Right-angled falls involve the construction of multiple waterfalls. The flow of water from the upper reaches needs to be divided so part continues at a higher level and cascades at intervals further downstream. Strategically placed rocks standing proud can divert water along a series of channels in a rock wall running alongside the main stream.

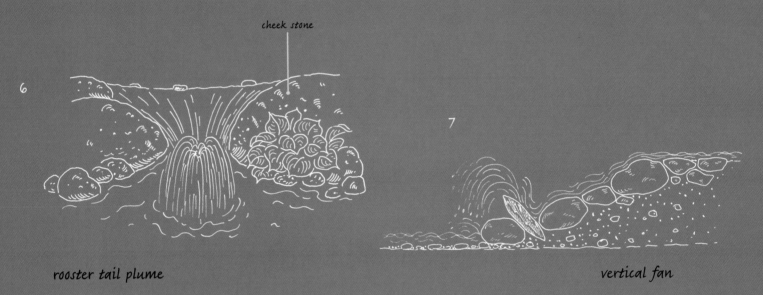

cheek stone

6

rooster tail plume

7

vertical fan

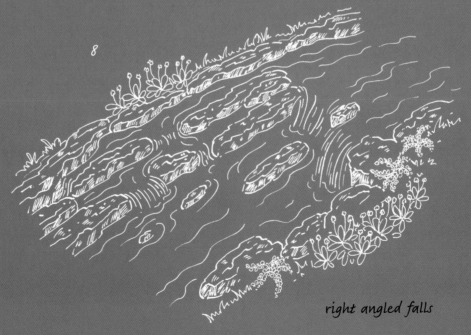

8

right angled falls

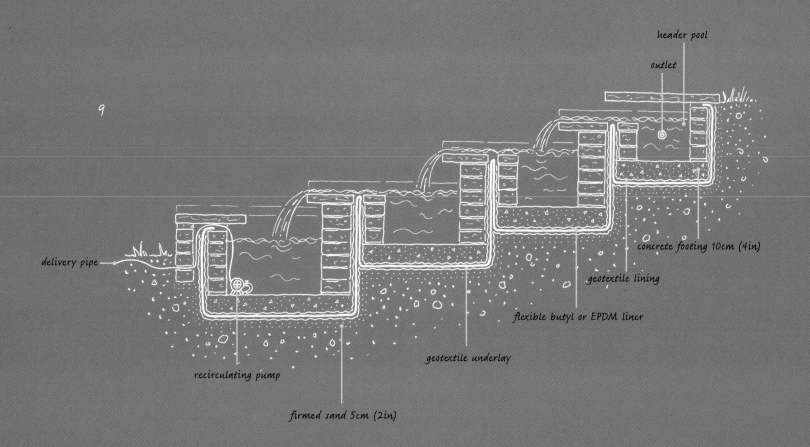

header pool

outlet

concrete footing 10cm (4in)

geotextile lining

flexible butyl or EPDM liner

delivery pipe

geotextile underlay

recirculating pump

firmed sand 5cm (2in)

9 ■ Formal waterfall with a recirculating system.

On a sloping site excavate a flight of steps. If the soil is soft pour on a concrete sub-base about 10cm (4in) thick to give stability, otherwise smooth the soil and firm a 5cm (2in) layer of sand over the surface. Now you can line the pools working from the bottom up and starting with the lowest reservoir. Once the lining is complete, cover the pool base with a concrete footing about 10cm (4in) deep to support walls of bricks or stone blocks. The liner and top layer of geotextile are folded up behind the back wall as shown, before the next pool is constructed. The upper pools are built in a similar manner, butting the walls close to the folded liner.

The pump is placed out of sight below an overhang in the lowest pool and the delivery pipe is passed through a duct in the walling, above the water level and below the coping, to a trench that runs alongside the waterfall to the header pool where the outlet is concealed. Finally flat spillstones are mortared in position to cap the walls and jut over the water. Check the level of the spillstones, they must be horizontal to ensure an even cascade.

WARNING: It is most important to employ a qualified electrician to install an outside power supply. The electricity supply must run in armoured cabling in a rigid plastic pipe buried at least 60cm (24in) below ground level, and a residual current device must be fitted to protect the system.

destination

natural *inspiration*

The water of the rushing course has its first real chance to warm up when it slows and broadens out into its final destination: a still, mirror-like pond, a rippling lake, the boiling water on a rocky sea shore, or even a smaller natural feature such as a rock pool. Sunlight gets to work on the water, instigating an immense and complex food chain, for now the water supports myriad life forms which abound in and around a pond. Flora and fauna flourish in the water, above it, and around the margins: dragonflies, birds and aquatic and moisture-loving plants.

I love the multiplicity of forms which natural ponds take. The reflections of the opposite banks with their varied contours, mossy rocks and plant life are among their chief attractions, and the variety of shorelines to be found around the world is immense. Rocky shorelines may be composed of fissured stratified ledges where plants can find footholds, or are formed from smooth, rounded boulders. There is often a strong demarcation between the dry land and the water as the edges fall away sheer with deep water lapping the sides of the rock. Above the rocky edge, among the crevices, highly specialized plants often find their ideal location and flourish.

In complete contrast are the marshy margins of inshore ponds. Here the transition from water to land may be virtually indiscernible. Great expanses of plants flourish in the wide margins and

right: Beneath the flickering surface with its colourful reflections there lies a highly specialized world containing many diverse creatures ranging from micro-organisms that coat the rocks to dragon-fly larvae and fish. We can shape this world so that its form suits our garden, and in it we can grow some of the loveliest natural species of plants or the most exotic hybrids ever produced by the gardener.

extend far into the deeper water. Botanically speaking, these lush marshy areas are among the richest places in the world and gorgeous rarities are sometimes the reward for the botanist who is prepared to search among the grasses.

Collectively termed 'wetlands', bogs, fens, swamps and marshes are some of the most exciting places in the world for the ecologist. Ranging as they do from the tundra to the tropics, they are host to a huge variety of flora and fauna, sustaining more life than most other ecosystems. Though covering less than six per cent of the earth's surface, they play a vital role in maintaining a stable global temperature. The wetlands also act as regulators, absorbing damaging floodwaters which they then release slowly into the river systems.

I built my first pond when I was sixteen. It was a poorly constructed affair, yet it became home to aquatic plants and pet fish and I loved it, despite its faults. Staring into the water I was enchanted: here was a world in miniature. The whole hierarchy of pond dwellers, from the larger predators to the microscopic bugs, competed for their water territories. I planted a water lily and eagerly awaited the first unfolding bud. The lines of an American Quaker poet, J. G. Whittier (1807–1892) in Frances Perry's inspirational *Water Gardening* (1938) came to mind:

There lingers not a breeze to break

The mirror which the waters make.

opposite: *Specialized plants can be discovered growing low amid the crevices of shoreline rocks.*
left: *Among bold stands of reeds, rushes and sedges there may be exciting moisture-loving plants.*
right: *The changing light deeply affects the mood of a pond.*
overleaf: *Water provides a backdrop to highlight tree and plant shapes and statuary.*

destination features

G iven enough space and unlimited funds, there is tremendous scope for ingenuity and originality in the design of pools, ponds and other areas of still water, and you can indulge your imagination to its utmost. There are also many questions to answer before you start planning. Will a pool have a recreational function or will it be purely ornamental? Do you want to contemplate water lilies or bask in the relaxing waters of a hot tub? The landscape will play an important role in your decision about what type of destination feature to choose, and will to some extent determine the structure and character of the feature.

below left: *Where space in the garden is limited, or a surprise feature or focal point is required, features such asa brimming basin or bird bath can be effective.*
right: *Beautiful, reflective shorelines can be simply created using the strong contrasting forms of rocks, boulders and mass plantings.*

If you have space for a large, informal pond, the existing contours of the garden could determine the shape and fashion the surrounds. Curved lines will be the most likely result and an undulating informal shape will be created. Where the contours are less restrictive, the shape of your pond can be as whimsical or bizarre as you like. Alternatively, you might like to consider a formal rectangular pond.

Small ornamental pools are among the easiest of features to integrate into a garden design. Any geometrically shaped pool can be incorporated into a formal design and the surrounds worked to suit. Conversely, in a wilder garden, you can design the pool to tie in stylistically with its surrounds. In gardens with a transitional design – where a formal area near the house gives way to a wilder zone further away – the pool can incorporate both elements: the part nearest the house or patio might be geometric in design while the far side could give way to rocks and mass plantings, perhaps of indigenous species. If the pool is situated further away from the house, a natural approach may be more appropriate. Alternatively,

far left: *A crisp edge defines formal or architectural details.*
left: *Even a small tank or pool will enliven a gloomy courtyard.*
below: *Swimming pools should be inviting – use planting to suggest fun and relaxation.*

you may want to create surprise in the garden by making an altogether unconventional statement. However, it is important first to learn the conventional rules of pool design so that you can then break them successfully.

Small pools usually look best in small gardens or in the intimate, enclosed areas of larger ones. Even a pond that occupies half an acre will look dwarfed in a large, open field, but in a woodland clearing it will appear as a great expanse of open space. In a tiny garden even the smallest pool becomes a dominant feature. Being smooth and flat, the surface of the water creates a strong contrast with the vertical forms of plants, trellis or buildings, and it is more conspicuous when surrounded by them. Conversely, if the pool is surrounded by flat, level grass, it will be less eye-catching.

A swimming pool need not be a conventional rectangle; clean-cut, geometric lines may complement a formal patio and the sharp angular lines of buildings. In some gardens a naturalistic design is more in keeping, with timber decking for

access and diving and large boulders set around it. Clumps of ornamental grasses planted beyond will blend this type of pool into the surrounding landscape. If space is in short supply, you might still be able to install a hot tub or jacuzzi, which can be made to blend in with any type of garden.

Bird baths are charming water features in the garden, bringing life, movement and song. They are an easy way of incorporating water into a small garden and can either be placed as focal points – perhaps as the centrepiece in a formal garden or potager – or partially hidden in a border to provide a surprise. Some are exquisite works of art such as the beautifully fashioned, shallow bronze pans held on elegant stalks, or the great flat dishes in dressed stone. Made of 'exposed aggregate' concrete, these latter types can be obtained for a more modest outlay. Even if you already have a small pond, a bird bath can be a wise adjunct, for if birds can be persuaded to take their dip in the bath, the cherished plants growing on the pond's margin might escape their attentions.

Pools need not be huge; even quite a small container can be sufficient for a miniature water feature. If you want to grow a fine specimen water plant you can improvise with wooden tubs, painted water tanks, old coppers and all manner of stone or timber-edged receptacles. Old stone troughs are particularly evocative. The larger ones measure some 2m (6ft) or more across, so simply by adding a mask or spout through which the water might pour into the trough, you can create a complete water garden with an antique rustic charm. One clump of arum lilies will improve the composition hugely and contrasts well with the angularity of the masonry.

The decision to incorporate a water feature into the garden is often one which has been discussed and deliberated upon for months – sometimes even years. It is a major step and the scale of the project can be daunting. You might therefore want to consider the help of a garden designer. Force of habit can lead us to accept incongruous elements in our immediate environment; we have become accustomed to that arbour, border or gazebo – even fond of it – although we realize that it is not necessarily in the ideal position. Sometimes a clean sweep is necessary and a trained design eye can spot this more easily. Most garden designers offer a wide range of services from giving design advice to designing, installing and planting the entire feature.

top: *Pools that are closely integrated into buildings should balance the lines and proportions of the structure. The design should work when viewed from inside and out.*
above: *The water of a pool may form part of a three-dimensional pattern contrasting in colour and shape with the adjacent surfaces.*

naturalistic pools

A 'natural' pool should nestle into the neighbouring landscape as though nature always intended it to be there. Although they are usually a bit bare immediately after construction, ponds start to blend into their environment surprisingly quickly. From the moment that the pond is full, the nearby trees, shrubs, buildings and sky are reflected in the water, linking it visually with its surroundings. Both marginal and aquatic plants establish themselves rapidly, and the feature looks settled in no time.

The easy availability of powerful excavating machinery and flexible liners makes the installation of a pond very tempting. Be careful, though, not to hurry the planning stage or the final result could be an artificial-looking pond that is difficult to alter.

For large-scale ponds you must first look carefully at the setting, Consider the shape of hills or valleys, wooded mounds or flat plains. Think about how your natural-looking pond can be sympathetically placed amid these features. Take particular note of any trees that you want to keep *in situ*, especially the elevation of their root balls, for there is little room for adjustment in soil levels around a tree. If you are working in a bog or marsh, be very careful not to raise or lower the water table, as this could be highly detrimental: flooding might well result in the loss of precious wild plants. Nevertheless, far from being restrictive, the constraints of local topography and flora often help the designer to reach a decision, by limiting the number of options available.

Having decided on the form of your feature, take note of the main structural features in the garden – mature trees, for example. The ultimate style of your scheme, whatever

far left: *A secluded pond, thickly planted around the margins and sheltered from the wind, provides a still surface for reflections and the lily pads.*
left: *Bleached rushes wait for a breeze to disperse their downy seed, while on the far side a lawn sweeps down right to the frozen water's edge.*
right: *Some natural ponds develop highly convoluted shore lines and are studded with small islands. These can result from the seeding of trees into mounds of sphagnum moss and can be particularly beautiful.*

its function or type, will be influenced by the existing buildings and surrounding landscape. Obviously the list will vary considerably, but you might include the garage, the wall around the kitchen garden, the woodland dell with its carpet of bluebells and orchids, and the specimen beech tree on the lawn. Half-close your eyes and imagine that everything else has disappeared: the little pathways, the shrubs, the old leaking fish pond. Now you have a clean canvas on which to create your new composition.

Smaller gardens which are part woodland and part lawn will also benefit from a pond. Reflecting the trees, a small pond can make a delightful focal point to walk to or just to sit beside. It may be completely surrounded by lawn, with thick clumps of emergent plants to provide a reflective backdrop. Alternatively, it may emulate a woodland pond in a rocky area with the stony margins reflected in the water.

The base of a bank is a natural setting for a pond. If the ground outside a house has been cut into to form a level patio, the resulting bank is an ideal spot for a small pond. The high ground behind the pond can be retained by rocks rising out of the water and there is great scope for a waterfall here. It is possible in this situation to have timber decking or paving coming up to the front edge of the pool without spoiling the natural effect.

Whereas the construction of large ponds and lakes is made significantly more difficult by steeply sloping sites, level and sloping sites alike provide ample opportunity for small naturalistic ponds. Town gardens, though tending to favour more formal water features, can also play host to natural-looking pools. Not all urban spaces are rigidly hemmed in by straight walls and fences, and even those that are can be softened by strategically planted trees and evergreen shrubs.

Inside the pond you will need to construct a ledge on which to place rocks or planting areas. Small beaches with judiciously placed large stones and pebbles will encourage frogs and provide birds with a place to spash or drink.

A pool which has irregular edges will blend in well in a naturalistic garden. Pebbles or gravel interspersed with larger boulders are excellent for creating this fluid outline, and the resulting beach-like effect could be extended into the garden – to form a gravel garden, perhaps. Strong architectural plants work well near paving or gravel: tall ornamental grasses like miscanthus make a tremendous visual impact rising gracefully from a bed of shingle; while non-invasive bamboo makes a fine rustling show. Phormiums and yuccas lend a Mediterranean flavour evocative of heat and sunshine. For an effective foliage contrast, try planting sprawling clumps of cistus and euphorbia. The softer, leafier appearance of these lower-growing species complements perfectly the powerful structures of the taller plants.

It is surprising what charming little oases of countryside can be created in the middle of dense urban development. Town dwellers who hanker for the pastoral can certainly look out on small informal pools adorned with clumps of water iris, and birds splashing on tiny pebble beaches. Modern plastic liners make the construction of small ponds very simple nowadays and the excavated soil can be used to vary the contours of the garden for a more naturalistic appearance. It is possible to create gentle rises and small hills with paths winding and dipping between them, and cover them in a profusion of beautiful scented plants. See blueprint 1, page 178.

The type of shoreline has to be considered in relation to the size, depth and underwater contours of the pool. Rocky shores can be used for all sizes of ponds, but the water will be deeper closer to the edge than you might expect. Large ponds might bear rocky outcrops, while it is possible for small ponds to accommodate rockwork around the edges without difficulty, on a ledge constructed around the perimeter. It is important that the bases of all the rocks remain underwater with only the attractive mossy parts visible above the surface, so considerable care will be needed in adjusting the rocks' elevations before you settle them into place. See blueprints 2, 3 and 4, page 179.

If you want to create a naturalistic planting scheme around the pond or if you have a pebble-and-sand beach surround, create a gently shelving edge, not exceeding a one-in-three slope. This will allow the soils and plants to stabilize in natural earth ponds, where the sides form a seal of mud

and silt; steeper sides would be unstable and would probably slide downwards. Fine particles of soil suspended in the water will also have more of a chance to settle down and form an effective waterproof coating.

Such a gentle slope would be impractical in a small pond, however, as the shelving edges would reach too far into the limited water area. However, most emergent and bog plants can be grown on shelves constructed around the perimeter in a manner similar to that described above for supporting rocks. The water depth for emergent plants can vary between 10cm (4in) and 30cm (12in). Bog plants are for the higher reaches where the soil is permanently moist but not necessarily submerged. In concrete or plastic-lined ponds you can build a shallow planting ledge which gives way to a steep or even vertical drop down to the bottom. This style of construction is impractical in natural earth or clay-lined ponds as the sides would be unstable.

opposite left: *A naturalistic pool can easily be tucked in beneath retaining walls and banks in town gardens. With cunning, the effect can be created that the water existed before the addition of the masonry.*
opposite right: *Rock gardens are shown off to good effect by the incorporation of naturalistic water features.*
above: *Tall plants enhance their own reflections by preventing breezes from ruffling the mirrored surface of the water.*

formal pools

above: *Reflection causes the gap between the edge and the water to seem greater than it really is.*
opposite: *A formal canal opens into a circular pool reflecting the sunset's glow and the silhouettes of the countryside beyond.*

The earliest artificial ponds were probably rectangular and based on the canal. The ends or the sides were sometimes simply embellished by being pulled outwards to form curves, called 'Roman-ended' pools. Once the basic canal shape was opened out into a pool it offered – within its symmetrical confines – many possibilities. By the beginning of the twentieth century the shape of most ponds was determined by the pure mathematics that had engendered Egyptian and Classical garden design and architecture, and the refined spiritual geometry of Islamic gardens.

A simple square, running parallel to the surrounding walls, still looks just as effective in a courtyard. The Spanish style of cloistered courtyard makes a perfect and elegant setting for a pond of this type. The octagon, a square with the corners

chopped off, is a logical progression; it looks more interesting and is easier to walk around, and it may be sunken, flush with the ground level or raised above it. Pushing the two pairs of opposite sides inwards to form slightly concave curvatures produces an interesting variation on the octagon.

In a formal garden situated away from buildings and surrounded by lawns and geometric flower beds, a curved or circular design is more appropriate. The round pond has the same elliptical shape, thinner or fatter, when viewed from any direction. An oval pond, meanwhile, will appear radically different when seen from different viewpoints. It may look perfectly circular from your bedroom window but will appear to resemble a cucumber when you walk past it.

In a small garden a formal pool works well as a centrepiece. More informal designs look better placed to one side, or as part of the boundary screen at the far end. If you plant a few choice specimens behind the pool, they will provide interesting reflections, create an attractive backdrop and disguise any artificial components that would spoil the illusion of naturalness. A semi-formal pond is very effective at the edge of a patio. Bounded on one side by decking or paving with a predominance of straight lines, the far side need not be angular but smoothly curved so that it will blend in well with a naturalistic garden.

Raised formal ponds are excellent for confined courtyards, town gardens and patios. They should have smooth coping in stone, slate or timber where you can sit and enjoy the reflections, plants and animal life in your pool and where you can put down cups or glasses to refresh yourself during your contemplations. See blueprints 5 and 6, page 180. Raised sides are safer, too, if there are small children or wheelchair users to consider.

The semi-raised pond can save work in town gardens where access is difficult, because the amount of material excavated when the pond is dug will be comparatively small. The surrounding walls form a large part of its depth, so only a little of the topsoil will have to be removed. This could be used on the site itself, possibly made up into one or more raised beds to complement the pond.

Whether the pond is raised or sunk, construction will be easier if you use a flexible liner rather than a concrete one to make the pond waterproof. Liners can be used to waterproof anything from dry stone walls to tufa blocks (which rapidly accommodate vegetation). Any size or shape of excavation can be lined but try to avoid sharp jutting edges and angular shapes. Gentle open curves are simpler to construct and easier on the eye than convoluted wriggling shapes, which could prove restless. Stone piers or more detailed rockwork can be added afterwards on top of the liner. See blueprints 7 and 8, pages 181–182.

A semi-formal pool might have a geometric pavement on one or more of its sides and a more irregular outline around the remainder of the water. A design like this will work particularly well if the pond is situated next to anything architectural, because the formal pavement may be treated in the same way as neighbouring terraces, walls or patios. Even if they were some distance apart, you could construct a pathway in a matching style to create a harmonious link between the house and your pool.

above: *Built into a terrace,*
a swimming pool can offer
breathtaking views as well as
seclusion. Swimming on the edge
of a mountain produces a safe
yet exhilarating feeling.
opposite: *Water at its most*
inviting; the temperature right;
the clarity perfect and it is just
waiting for you. This is the goal.

swimming pools

Although they can be expensive to install and have running costs, swimming pools bring ample rewards. Not only are they a suitable focus for social gatherings, they also enable you to take exercise and improve your health, or to relax and wind down at the end of a stressful day. Regular checks on the clarity of the water will make for easier maintenance and save time and money in the long run. Specialist contractors can be engaged to look after the pool so that you have little to worry about regarding the mechanics. There are cleaning machines and devices that monitor almost every aspect of pool care – from acidity to temperature. These can inject or adjust whatever is needed automatically, leaving you free to just enjoy the pool at your leisure.

Swimming pool design opens up many exciting possibilities. As well as cosy indoor and sunny outdoor pools, some owners opt for the best of both worlds and run their pools from inside to out. Outdoor swimming pools offer the greatest range of design options. It is feasible to create a pool for every conceivable situation and taste.

Siting the pool requires careful thought, there are a number of factors that must be weighed up. Remember that a certain amount of noise and boisterousness is an inescapable part of pool life, particularly where young people are involved. The luxury of a pre-breakfast dip just outside the living room might seem appealing, but siting the pool so close to your house might mean that your peaceful Sunday afternoons are disturbed. Does the thought of towels and damp swimsuits left in the conservatory depress you? If so, you might consider siting the pool further from the house with an adjacent pool room for changing and storing pool toys.

Climate is a major consideration when it comes to designing an outdoor pool. In the cooler northern regions well-sheltered secluded pools will be called for, surrounded by high hedges or enclosed by walls. Choose a sunny position and keep the pool as small as possible for ease and economy of heating. If they suit the situation, rectangular pools are probably best because covering them (sensible in anything less than a Mediterranean climate) is easy and relatively cost-effective.

In Mediterranean regions and hotter countries further south swimming-pool design can be much more extravagant. Here the aim is to keep the water cool and refreshing. Some of the loveliest pools use 'borrowed scenery'. They are built on high terraces overlooking deep valleys, distant hills and sometimes the ocean. When you swim in one it feels as if you are swimming on the edge of limitless space, particularly when the pool water actually spills over the edge on the valley side in a continuous smooth sheet into a trough below, rendering the pool edge invisible. The recirculation system can be arranged to incorporate an ornamental cascade or waterfall that can either feed into or pour out of the pool.

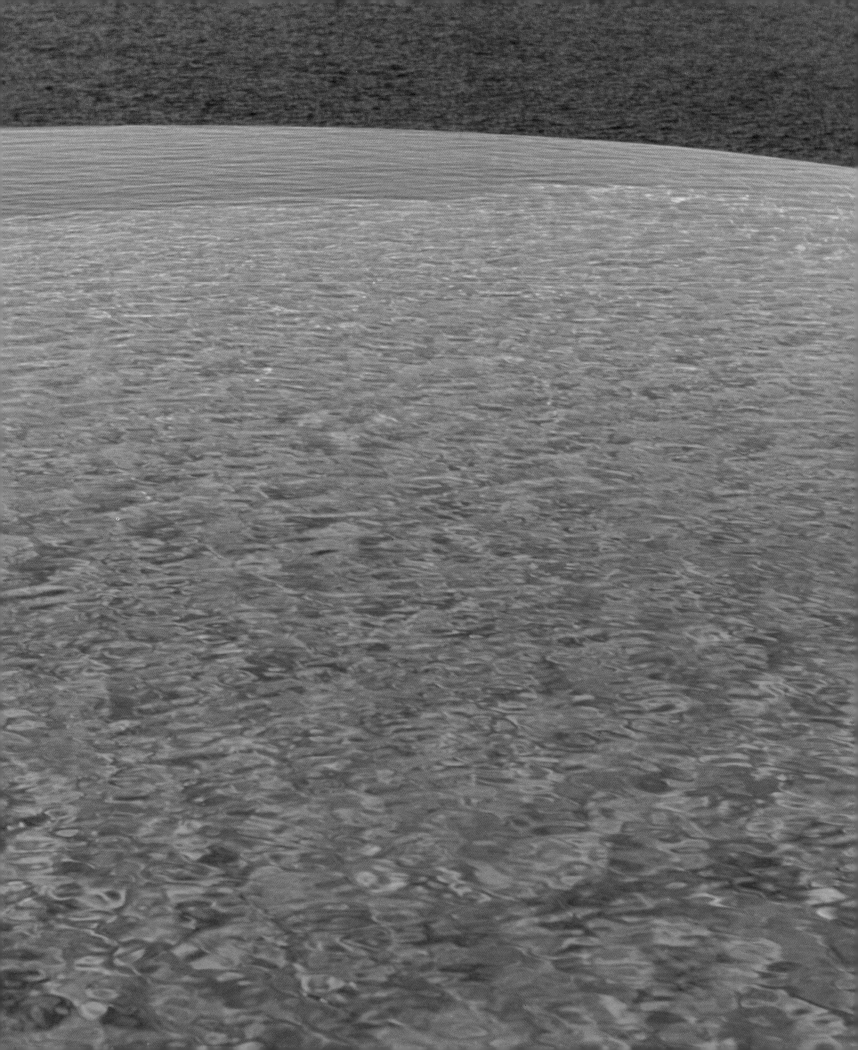

The idea of an indoor–outdoor pool is tempting in any climate. Sliding glass doors will afford you the necessary protection if it is cool and windy; you may bask at your ease and still enjoy looking at the garden outside. In some pools a permanent screen just touches the surface of the water and keeps out the cold air. It is great fun to duck underneath it and pop up

above right: *A swimming pool can be enjoyed in almost any available space in or around the house.*

above: *Seen from a distance the deep clear water of a swimming pool will take on the colour of the sky. This ability makes a pool a useful feature to link visually the house, sea, lake and sky.*

in the great outdoors. Architecturally such designs can add exciting new dimensions to a building: if space is limited, for example, the pool can be extended to occupy a flat roof.

Though not strictly a garden feature, a glass-encased indoor pool is worthy of inclusion here, for building an open pool in the garden will probably involve the same type of considerations – how to hide the structure with planting or incorporate it into the overall design. Something more decorative could be constructed: perhaps a roof in glass or perspex to act as the pool's cover. To my mind, an indoor pool in anything but the coolest climate cannot compare with an outdoor one. In cold conditions, however, the indoor pool comes into its own. You may plunge into the water at

any season of the year and enjoy the freedom of movement engendered by warm water. Humidity and temperature must be well controlled to prevent the walls and ceiling from dripping with condensation.

The ornamentation of a swimming pool will be dictated by its style. Is the pool composed of free fluid shapes to integrate perfectly into a wild garden? Is the pool angular, with strong geometric lines? Is it built along strict classical lines to emulate an ancient pool? Whatever the concept, there is an enormous range of tiles and stones on the market now from which to create the perfect finish for the rustic, formal or modern pool of your dreams. Where there is strong sunlight opt for terracotta, coloured stone or timber decking rather than the glaring white so prevalent around pools until quite recently.

The functional requirements of the pool allow for a range of decorative effects. The pool will have a return flow of water from its filtration plant and part or all of this could be used for ornamental purposes. In a formal setting the water could be re-introduced into the pool through a wall-mounted mask or simple stone spout. A free-standing stone could take the place of the wall. The water might fall directly into the pool or cascade down into a series of stone or ceramic bowls or troughs. It may be conducted through a rill with waterfalls or

from the mouth of an urn placed on its side. A water curtain falling into the pool is enormous fun for children to play under, but perhaps the most exciting feature for a pool is a cave or grotto where the water cascades through part of the roof or across the mouth. An area of shallower water here would be safe for children and provide somewhere to rest and enjoy the effects of the falling water.

Warm water re-entering from a lip in the wall of an adjacent hot tub or spa makes a functional and attractive feature to a pool. The spa itself should be constructed in the same manner and from the same materials as the pool itself to ensure that it does not look like it has been added on as an afterthought, but is an integral part of the pool.

The scope for planting will necessarily be limited in any type of pool meant for swimming in. Planting in the water itself would be inappropriate and generally unhygienic, and,

in any case, plants would not be able to survive in water that had been chemically treated. With a little imagination, there are still plenty of interesting opportunities for planting afforded by the pool's immediate environment. I have come across several beautiful swimming pools where there are containers constructed of the same material as the pool itself which rise up out of the water. Here palms and yuccas can tower above the water, growing happily surrounded by a mulch of smooth pebbles. There is plenty of scope in the area around the pool for planters of every description, both permanent or temporary. Remember, though, to position them well out of the way of children's play areas.

The large reflective surface area of a swimming pool makes it ideal for displaying sculptures and interesting *objets trouvés*. Figurative sculptures such as Graeco-Roman nymphs suit a formal classical pool. Some sculpture brings a touch of humour to the poolside, as in a French pool I know that sports two life-size bronze nudes. One is luxuriating in a teak seat, her bronze sunglasses lying close by. Her companion stands on the other side of the pool, drying himself off with a towel. Life-size bronzes such as these, however, are extremely expensive and do not suit every setting. The most timeless and serene formal pool I know is one which has severe and pure classical proportions. Restrained to the point of minimalism, at one end it has a great upraised millstone with a hole through the centre recalling the great monoliths of prehistoric times in its simplicity and dignity.

The furniture with which you surround your pool will not only be functional, but will also be as important a part of the feature as the sculpture, rocks or plants surrounding it. A curved stone, metal or wooden bench can make an attractive and useful addition to the poolside.

informal swimming pools

The sea is the ultimate swimming pool, especially when it is crystal clear and as warm as a tepid bath. There is probably no better place to learn to swim than in warm sea water, for the buoyancy of the salt water and the warmth combine to relax the learner and dispel fear. A gently shelving beach encourages the young or inexperienced swimmer to enjoy the water without ever getting out of their depth. The water tempts you to peer beneath the surface, at darting shoals of small fish, seaweed waving gently in the current and the rippling sands and shells on the sea bed. The bliss of swimming in these conditions produces a sense of freedom which must be akin to flying.

A clear warm lake in summer can produce sensations almost as delicious as the sea – that wonderful refreshing feeling of being at one with nature – but it lacks the salt water's buoyancy and the dynamic lifting movement of the waves. Many large public pools now use wave-making machines to simulate the energy of the sea indoors, recreating the sense of adventure and fun provided by the waves.

The seashore, or any other beautiful natural pool, may act as a model for an informal swimming pool. Attractive outcrops of rock can be incorporated on ledges around the perimeter of the pool – high ones to use as diving platforms and lower, flatter ones for sunbathing on – and water from the pumping system can be returned over a rocky waterfall. You can build gently shelving beaches in sand-coloured cement, and timbering decks provides a sympathetic and practical hard surface. The artificial bright blue or tiled effect of a conventional pool can be replaced by either a black or dark grey lining. Black is gentle and restful on the eye and creates the impression of a deep body of water underneath. It also provides a surface that is highly reflective – for a naturalistic pool the ever-changing reflection of the sky and the surroundings is much more appropriate than insistent bright blue tiling.

Any tendency to a stark dominating regularity in the surrounds of an informal pool can be broken by incorporating beautiful natural boulders, but care must be taken to make rockwork appear convincing. It should rise out of the water or else be set back and rise up out of the ground like a natural outcrop. Rocks perched on the rim of a pool look artificial and could be dangerous. Try to make the pool blend with the surroundings, by linking the rock work and planting at the edges with the rest of the garden.

The same rules for planting apply here as for more formal pools. It is easier and generally more hygienic to concentrate on planting around the poolside rather than within the pool itself. There are still plenty of interesting possibilities for naturalistic planting at the edges of the pool, using plants such as low grasses, yuccas and miscanthus.

opposite: Almost any effect imaginable can now be created in a swimming pool. Sandy beaches, rocky outcrops, islands with palm trees and waterfalls are now easily to obtain

above: A special place for the pool – warm, secluded and surrounded by an ocean of scented plants to increase the pleasure of swimming.

design uses

From an engineering point of view there are only a few places where it is not possible to place a pond or swimming pool, offering enormous scope when using the feature in the overall garden design. As regards scale, I have yet to find a pond which looks too large for the house and garden. Historically, after all, people built their homes beside existing lakes to enjoy the pleasures of a lakeside residence. Some houses are still built on promontories and are virtually surrounded by water. Some are built on tiny islands, either in lakes or off the coast; lake island dwellings, in a secluded and attractive environment are particularly popular in America.

right: An expanse of water amid architectural structures will enhance the scene in many ways. The simple level plane contrasts with the vertical structural elements. Complexity is added by the moving shapes and colours created by the reflections.
left: *A tiny rock pool, half hidden by vegetation, will appeal to wildlife.*

Given sufficiently large machinery and enough imagination and daring, it is possible to sculpt the landscape with as much whimsy and inventiveness as a sculptor might use to produce a bronze or wood carving. Earth and water can be worked to symbolic or decorative effect. The main or even sole reason for building a pond might be to reflect a particularly attractive feature in it. A clear and dark surface will mirror magnificent trees, fine buildings or sculpture to perfection. It will intensify a focal point and bring life, drama and movement to more static surroundings.

Many ponds are built to provide a haven for wildlife, either creatures within the water such as frogs, or areas for birds at the edges. Others are constructed to increase the impact, and affect the musicality of the sound of water falling down into them from fountains or waterfalls.

Some of the most beautiful and dramatic landscapes are those where rock and water come together. You may decide that you want to recreate a few of nature's infinitely diverse manifestations in your own garden. If this is so, then you must

along one or both vistas. Never underestimate the effect of perspective. Mark out the shape with a rope, hose or marker on the ground and observe it from all angles before you embark on any excavations. The shape should appear to sit comfortably within the existing contours of the environment.

The centre of a small formal garden or a potager is often a good place to position a formal pond. A small garden is not at all dissimilar to an enclosed compartment of a large garden which has been divided into many different 'rooms'. More informal designs tend to look better when situated over to one side or at the far end of a small garden. Here they can be backed up by interesting planting which forms part of the boundary screen. A few choice plants behind the pond will provide reflections on the water's surface, create an attractive backdrop for the feature, and will also serve to

above: *Sometimes the water may seem to be part of a solid structure, especially when it appears to be black and the surface is highly reflective.*

right: *Planters may form an important part of the design. These can be built to balance the open water or create patterns in the same structural materials as the surrounds.*

ensure that your scheme harmonizes with the basic landscape of the area. The direction of the sunlight, viewpoints, access routes and safety are all vital considerations as you ponder the design for your pool. Having noted all these important factors, you should be able to arrive at a scheme which is tailored to your requirements, and one that works well within the existing surroundings.

A pond can be used effectively as a focal point to enhance a particular vista. The crossing point of two paths is another excellent position to place a pond and the effect can be strengthened if it is extended to form ornamental canals

disguise any visible artificial components which would otherwise spoil the illusion of naturalness.

The edge of a patio is an excellent place for a semi-formal pool – one that is bounded by the straight lines of pavement or decking on one side while the far side merges with a naturalistic garden. The result will appear to be a long-established natural pond which has been reduced by the need to construct walking or sitting areas on the side next to the house. The obviously man-made work accentuates the natural appearance of the informal parts of the pond. Smooth stone flags or timber planks are excellent edgings for patio ponds, being both solid and inviting to walk on. Brickwork can be used to echo that of the adjacent walls but is much more demanding at the construction stage, being smaller and less stable than a plank or large slab.

The patio or deck is a good place to position a raised pool. Small pools can even be constructed on balconies or roofs provided that the safe weight limit for the structure is not exceeded. It is always useful to make the coping of a pond suitable for sitting on for this will provide much needed extra seating in a small area. An existing wall niche with a stone seat will make an excellent place to site a small formal pond. A nearby garden chair or even a simple log bench will invite one to pause and take 'time out' to contemplate the water, plants and pond creatures.

Naturalistic ponds in larger gardens make good surprise features. It is fun to come across one unexpectedly upon rounding the bend, or to suddenly discover a still and silent woodland pool in a glade or clearing, out of sight and sound of the house.

left: *Pools may be designed as deliberate interruptions en route round a garden. These pauses force one to stop and view the scene, and then take a roundabout path to view other parts of the garden.*
above: *Paths leading to bridges and stepping stones are an invitation to cross over at a particular point.*

using reflections

The reflection of a cloud on the surface of a pond may be the first inkling you have of its existence. People tend to look down and often do not notice what is happening above their heads.

The reflection we see is the image of the object viewed from the level of the water's surface. This means that what we see mirrored in the water is taken from a lower viewpoint than when we look directly at the building or object. This can play some interesting tricks. I remember one pool in which I could see the reflection of a golden weather vane against a patch of blue sky surrounded by foliage. To my surprise, when I looked up it was not visible. From where I stood the weather vane, was hidden behind a horizontal branch and the building on which it was mounted was hidden from view.

The image reflected in dark still water often looks clearer than the object itself. With bridges and decks, the gap between the underside of the construction and the surface of the water will permit the underside to be reflected and very much on view. It should therefore be carefully designed, and any unsightly pipes running beneath decking should be well disguised or boxed in out of sight. The space between decking and water should be kept to a minimum because the reflection will double the height optically and make the structure look too high or too bulky. The same principle applys to walls and pond rims. What may seem minimal at the design stage could appear massive in elevation, doubled by its own reflection.

A well-constructed bridge, on the other hand, will look beautiful mirrored in the water. The oriental arched 'half-moon' bridges can look like a full moon when reflected. The dark undersides of stone arched bridges and overhanging rocks become illuminated with fascinating darts of sunlight reflected upwards from ripples in the water. Gazebos, temples, summerhouses and pavilions all make wonderful subjects for reflections in larger pools. Careful positioning is required to ensure that the reflections are seen to best effect from the intended viewing point.

I once constructed a circular pool specifically to reflect a piece of sculpture erected on a hill behind it. Brimful and still, surrounded by mown grass, the pool resembled a round mirror on the lawn. The sculpture was specially designed with reflections in mind and it had fine details on the undersides of projecting parts. Pond and sculpture combined perfectly to create the final piece.

previous page: *Curious effects in perspective, reminiscent of an Escher drawing, can be created by altering the geometry of a pool outline.*

below: *Clear dark reflective water takes on the myriad colours of its surroundings.*

right: *Dawns and sunsets are particularly beautiful when their reflections are added in a pond or lake.*

Objects and plants can be combined to form intriguing compositions that are enhanced by the symmetry caused by reflection. Using combinations of contrasting outlines will increase the degree of interest. Large pots, gnarled driftwood, graceful grasses, bent old olives, and even antique farm machinery, can all be used to great effect, their images mirrored in the calm, reflective water.

Slender reeds, iris and bamboos create a vertical element whose reflection appears to penetrate deep into the water. The rounded leaves of petasites or the great *Gunnera manicata* throw their reflections onto the water and provide a strong contrast with the tall slender species. The whole effect is further dramatized by the smooth horizontal surface of the still water.

When positioning plants, sculptures and other objects for reflection, it is worth taking some trouble to find the ideal spot by moving them around and observing the reflections from different viewpoints and at different times of the day. 'Reflections' can mean mirrored images, but it can also mean quiet tranquil thoughts. Both meanings are contained in a deep still pool, for the water works powerfully on the emotions and brings about a feeling of calm and well-being. Colour adds to the drama, and in summer the green canopies

of the trees are faithfully reproduced on the water's surface in great pools of emerald and jade. Autumn brings brilliant golds, crimsons and russets, stunning when viewed against a clear blue sky reflected on the surface of the water. Nowhere is this spectacular display more vibrant than in New England, USA, where the sugar maples (*Acer saccharum*), nyssas, liquid ambars and red maples (*Acer rubrum*) flaunt themselves in a sumptuous fiery annual exhibition.

In my view the pool as a mirror is at its most beautiful during the 'short death' of the winter months. The stark greys and silvers of denuded, skeletal trees and shrubs create dramatic reflections. The monochromatic greys provide a perfect foil for more brilliant plants such as willows and dogwoods with their coloured stems and white-barked birches. These unexpected bursts of colour are even more luminous following a fall of snow, when every twig sports a white cap and the winter sky provides a backdrop of vivid glacial blue.

Venture out to the far side of your pond and look back towards the house. If the water is still unfrozen the house will be vividly displayed as on a screen, every detail sharply defined. The mirroring surface provides the vital link, fusing house and garden into one entity.

left: *Leaning trees can create chevron images when reflected in still water.*
below: *The slightest ripple or breeze will wave the stems of reeds and other delicate emergent plants, and also make their reflections shimmer on the surface.*

above: The reflection of any vertical structure that is not completely plumb will form an angle with the surface. Although demanding, this phenomenon can open up many varied design possibilities.

opposite: Viewed from the far side of the pool the house can create exciting and inviting images on the water's surface.

reflecting light into the house

Even before shrines and temples were built in ancient Greece, a cover was built for the sacred springs which gushed out of the earth to maintain their purity. In Athens around 530 bc the venerated Callirrhoe was made into a fountain where water spouted from nine lions' masks. Increasingly complex structures were constructed as time went on and in 13 bc, Marcus Agrippa ordered the building of a complex in Rome that combined the public hot baths, a sumptuous garden, a library and an eating area. A belief in water's health-giving properties has secured its incorporation into both domestic and public architecture since ancient times.

The use of water close to a building is undoubtedly beneficial to those living or working inside. Though silent, a still pool makes its presence felt by reflecting light into the interior. If you are planning to have a pool close to your house, take careful note of the position of the sun. In the northern hemisphere, a pond on the south side will throw wonderful rippling darts of light on the walls and ceilings of the upper floors, the full strength of the sunlight being reflected up from the water's surface. If the pool is still the reflection will form a great square of brilliance, but as soon as the water starts to move, so the light will dance too. If you have a fountain, the reflected light will create a living work of art as the reflected ripples form constantly changing patterns. A pool on the north side of the house will be in shadow for a large part of the day. The sun shining over the rooftop, however, will be reflected into the pool from any buildings or trees on the far side of the pool, then reflected from the pool's surface into north-facing rooms. The northern light is a constant even light, favoured by artists in their studios. By placing a pool to the north you may even be able to take advantage of a neighbour's trees to illuminate your patio or brighten a gloomy room. It is a good position for a pool if you are planning to place a piece of sculpture beyond the water.

If your pool lies to the east, you could wake to rippling patterns of light on the bedroom ceiling. It is in the evening, however, that a pond situated in the east shows its best colours. Meanwhile, a pool situated to the west will create a warm afterglow in the house as the colours of the sunset are reflected back off the water surface into the interior. When they are illuminated by the evening sun, waterside plants such as scarlet and golden-stemmed dogwoods and willows create breathtaking reflections.

linking house and garden

Few have exploited the juxtaposition of architectural features and brimming pools better than the Islamic garden designers, and no-one has evoked the magical effects of the reflected image to better purpose. To all appearances as solid and substantial as the original stone, the reflected buildings are as intangible as the fairytale palaces decribed in tales such as the *Arabian Nights*. The interplay between liquid and solid, is dramatic and pleasurable and clear pools are often designed to run right up to, around or even through the building.

If this effect is too starkly architectural for your liking, it is possible to soften the result with judicious aquatic planting. Tubs of papyrus and lotus thrive in hot climates and plants such as water lilies and rushes grow well in colder regions.

The more we learn about the therapeutic value of light and space and the psychological benefits derived from natural colours, scents, sounds and even from animals, the more important it becomes to break down those barriers that divide our interior and exterior living spaces. Water can play a crucial role here, being equally at home in both. I have already described how swimming pools can be built to run from inside a building to out and you can construct a fishpond in the same way. This is a well-established practice in Japan where ponds of this nature are home to the highly prized Koi carp. The fish cruise between the garden and the sitting room as the fancy takes them, or as the weather dictates; allowing the owner to enjoy the sight of them both indoors and out. A solid wall or window or a movable screen can be used extending right down from the ceiling to thewater's surface, to prevent draughts from entering the house and stop all the heat from escaping.

Swimming pools can also be constructed to flow into and out of the house, permitting swimmers both the pleasure of outdoor swimming in finer weather and the luxury of protection in cooler weather. Like the Moorish and Spanish-style houses of old, where the cloistered courtyards and the colonnades gave the impression that the house and the garden were combined, so the water unites the two and it is impossible to tell where the one of them ends and the other begins. Are you outside when you swim beneath the eaves or when you emerge into the bright sunlight?

These indoor–outdoor pools remind me of the paintings of Russell Flint, whose scantily clad lovelies drape themselves around ancient Roman baths amid old plaster and columns.

Do not site islands in the middle of the pond or in the longest vista. Keep this open to enhance the feeling of distance and to maximize the expanse of the water and thus the area for reflections. A group of three islands of varying sizes makes for a harmonious composition. On a small scale the group could comprise one little island with some plants to provide cover for wildfowl, one island consisting of a large rock, and the third a smaller rock sticking up out of the water.

In formal pools the islands may be barren and composed of the same materials as those used in the pool surrounds. Low platforms of paving approached by stepping stones are great fun and create pleasing geometric patterns. They are good settings for sculpture, which will be mirrored to perfection in the surrounding water. If the surrounds are of timber rather than masonry, the island could be constructed of wooden planking and approached by similar bridges designed to conform with the style of the pool.

It is exhilarating to walk the springy decking beside a pond and hear your footsteps ringing aloud on the hollow timbers. The thrill is intensified when you stride out upon a landing stage, defying the deep water which glints up at you through the gaps in between the planks. Decking and landing stages work well with both formal and natural pools. Decking makes a pond appear larger and more imposing. Because timber is a natural substance, it makes an excellent transitional material between a formal timber-decked patio area and a naturalistic pool extending into an informal or wild garden.

Decks and landing stages must be well built and look and feel safe. Do not use rustic timbers with the bark left on the wood as they can rot away or be eaten by woodworm under the bark and suddenly give way underneath you.

The strict geometry of timber decking makes it a good foil for plants. A landing stage looks most inviting peeping out through tall rushes, water iris or the graceful cyperus. On the dry land side miscanthus, pampas and similar tall grasses set the horizontal lines of the boarding off to perfection.

opposite: *A landing stage in a natural pool is immensely inviting. It provides a firm dry standing area, a good vantage point to view both shoreline and water and a convenient place to board a boat.*
above: *Timber decks and causeways are fun to walk or lounge on. They provide additional recreational areas and can link inaccessible parts that lay beyond the water. A floating causeway has the added attraction for children of undulating as they run across.*

islands and decking

If your pond or swimming pool is large enough you may want to incorporate one or more islands – as havens for wildlife, as settings for planting or sculpture, or simply to punctuate the water's surface. They must however be planned with care. By permitting a stretch of water to be dominated by one or more islands you risk spoiling the very thing you are trying to create – an attractive view of the water.

Viewed in perspective and from a low vantage point , islands can drastically obscure your view of the water. Even though they may rise only a few centimetres above the water's surface, their plant life will veil the water beyond. Keep them as small as possible because as their vegetation encroaches outwards they will expand. That unassuming islet you created a couple of years ago may be making determined strides to unite itself with its companion islands a few feet away, and sooner or later you could end up with no pond at all.

surface and underwater lighting

Well-planned lighting will enable you to enjoy your pool at night and will lend it a new and exciting character. Boulders, plants and ornaments whose form appears flattened and whose colours appear faded in sunlight, become dramatic, many-hued, shadowed shapes when picked out in lamplight. Angle the lights low, and long atmospheric shadows will be cast. Shine the lights onto plants and rocks rather than the water, and you will be rewarded with vivid reflections on the dark surface, which shimmer and ripple whenever a breeze blows. The paraphenalia of lighting and cables should be concealed and made from dull materials so they do not attract attention. Aim for subtle, restrained effects – there is no romance in a glare resembling a football stadium at night.

Underwater lighting reveals a hidden world beneath the surface, where brightly coloured fish flit like birds through viridian forests of undulating water plants. Magical effects can be created by placing lamps beneath fountains or behind waterfalls. It is necessary periodically to clean off the mud and algae which settles on submerged lighting equipment.

Indoor swimming pools reflect the ceiling and this can be decorated to great effect. Like the fairytale rock formations reflected in subterranean lakes, a pool can reflect a grotto or a galaxy of stars. It could duplicate half of a symmetrical shape like a traditional Chinese half-moon bridge, so the reflected image and the original shape meet to form a whole. I once swam in a pool whose deep blue barrel-vaulted ceiling was spangled with hundreds of tiny lights, some of them fibre-optic clusters. Submerged lighting intensifies the clarity of the water by illuminating the bottom. The impression is of diving into a pool of shimmering light. When swimming at night, if the humidity is low, clouds rise from the pool like an enchanted cauldron, an effect enhanced by judicious surface lighting.

The installation of lighting and the power supply should be undertaken by a qualified electrician.

planting

The most conspicuous part of a pool is its edging and its treatment is therefore of the utmost importance. The planting here can make or mar the finished appearance of the whole environment. It can mean the difference between owning a pond which is easy to maintain or being tied down to a difficult and time-consuming programme of weeding, thinning and transplanting. It can transform the pool into a pleasure to look at or make it untidy and unattractive. And, it plays a major role in creating a healthy and thriving ecosystem both inside the pool itself and in the surrounding area.

right: To create as much year round interest as possible, use a range of emergent and moisture loving plants and waterside shrubs. Aim for effective foliage and stem contrasts and punctuate with flowering plants. Even dead stems will be an attractive foil for harbingers of spring like the marsh marigold.

The edging will vary according to the degree of formality or informality of the pool. Some pools may be surrounded by a hard architectural edge forming a distinct barrier between areas of pool and garden planting. Beyond the edge where all planting is on dry land any appropriate plant could be chosen.

Strong sinuous plants like the arum lily will counteract the stark angularity of more formal ponds and soften the hard outlines. Alternatively, the horizontal element in formal pools can be echoed by using plants like prostrate junipers, whose evergreen boughs will fan out across the stone edging. Create a contrast by planting one of the graceful soaring grasses like *Miscanthus sinensis* 'Variegatus' on ledges inside the pond.

Around swimming pools where flat expanses of paving tend to predominate, I like to see cushions of plants spreading out across the stone. With its aromatic silver or green foliage, cheerful yellow buttons and compact shape, santolina is one of my favourites. Another is cistus, which is drought-resistant, evergreen, sometimes aromatic, and bears attractive papery flower. The invigorating spicy fragrance of lavender (*Lavandula*)

and box (*Buxus*) fill the air in warmer weather, reminiscent of the balmy heat of the Mediterranean for those who live in cooler climates. Make good use of walls or trellises around swimming pools by growing scented climbers like honeysuckle or jasmine or delicious thornless blackberries. I know a pool owner who invites visitors to help themselves to the grapes which clothe his poolside trellis.

The best way to grow water plants in a formal pond is on a shallow (25–30cm/9–12in deep) ledge. Here you can establish strategic clumps of emergent plants. Use powerful shapes which will hold their own against the strong straight lines of the edging.There is a wide range of plants to suit cool temperate or tropical conditions. True bullrush (*Schoenoplectus lacustris*) and Japanese bullrush (*S. lacustris* 'Albescens') make fine upstanding clumps for colder countries. Giant marsh marigold (*Caltha polypetala*) with its rounded leaves provides a pleasing contrast. For less frost-prone areas cannas make a tall elegant display with an exciting tropical air and spectacular bright flowers. See blueprint 9, page 182.

above: *Sometimes the yellow and white skunk cabbages will cross pollinate to produce a lovely cream hybrid.*

right: *Almost duplicating the leaf shapes, the goldfish cluster together in the shade.*

opposite left: *Thick growing emergent plants can soften solid structures like dry stone walls.*

opposite right: *A delightful interplay of shapes is produced by mixing the flat pads of water lilies with the slender cylindrical stems of reeds and iris.*

For a lower and denser effect plant the pickerel weed (*Pontederia cordata*) which has blue flower spikes and glossy heart-shaped leaves. In hot areas there is little to beat the cool evergreen luxuriance of paper rush (*Cyperus papyrus*) with its radial inflorescences atop lofty stems. They remind me of fireworks. Where space is limited you can substitute *C. haspan*.

The gradually sloping perimeters of more naturalistic ponds provide a variety of situations for planting, ranging from shallow water through mud to dry land. Here it is possible to grow a diversity of flora collected from marshes, swamps and fens from the tundra to the tropics. These plants are usually very adaptable for the most part as in their native habitats they would have had to contend not only with the encroachment of other species but also with occasional floods and droughts. Exception to this rule are the Asiatic primulas and some bog- and moisture-loving plants which do not tolerate drastic fluctuations in water levels. Many emergent plants, however, are happy to spread from the areas under 10cm (4in) of water to a depth of 30cm (12in) or more. Moreover, they are happy to clamber up onto practically dry land. Such plants are easy to grow and many are graceful. However, they tend to have greedy spreading roots and require plenty of plenty of space or shallow areas next to deep areas into which they cannot spread. Although these plants are vigorous, their roots have a beneficial effect on the health and clarity of the water. Examples of this type of plant are the common or Norfolk reed (*Phragmites australis*) and greater and lesser reedmace or cat's tail (*Typha latifolia* and *T. angustifolia*) Some, like the beautiful purple loosestrife (*Lythrum salicaria*), are banned in some areas where they have become a rampageous weed. In the British Isles *Crassula helmsii*, marketed as *Tilea recurva,* is starting to have a serious impact on the balance of flora. It creeps inexorably, forming a thick mat over moist soil. Avoid it.

There are some beautiful plants which will limit themselves to growing in shallow water and rarely become a nuisance. The flowering rush (*Butomus umbellatus*) is one. This has large rosy pink umbels and reddish buds borne above slender stems 1.2m (4ft). The lovely water iris seldom rampage and come in all colours. Some, like the blue-flowered *Iris laeviagata* 'Variegata' even have attractive striped foliage. It is simply a matter of selecting a colour scheme and making sure the water depth is right for the species chosen.

The strip of damp soil surrounding the pond is ideal for those moisture-loving plants which dislike water over their crowns. Some of the species which tolerate deeper water will compete for this space also and this is a reason for excluding them. Many plants normally associated with the herbaceous border – ligularias, lobelias and hostas – will flourish even better in damp soil. It is the ideal spot for those most showy of moisture-loving species, the candelabra primulas. The enormous *Gunnera manicata* finds sufficient moisture here to unfold its jagged leaves to full effect and the stately royal fern (*Osmunda regalis*) will unfurl endearing croziers in spring. False spikenard (*Smilacina racemosa*), fresh green and gracefully arching, scents the air with its lily-of-the-valley perfume and rubs shoulders with the vivid blue meconopsis which enjoy a similar slightly acid, moist soil.

You can create a suitable habitat for bog- and moisture-loving plants alongside a pool. The simplest method is to leave a wide ledge 25–30cm (9–12 in) deep when you construct the pool. If you are using a liner, cover this with topsoil sloping gradually from soil level around the outer edge to a shallower covering towards the centre of the pool. If the pond is small and the ledge is too narrow to achieve a gentle slope, use sandbags, rocks or rounded stones to form a barrier at the bottom of the earth bank to prevent the heaped-up soil on the ledge sliding into the water. In formal ponds this can be constructed of brick or stone. Natural earth or clay ponds will only require a covering of good soil over the shallows to enable the plants to establish. Alternatively, you can create a marshy place for them using a flexible liner and a perforated hose or control tank to supply water. See blueprint 10, page 183.

Given the choice of emergent plants, the area just above the waterline gives you every opportunity to blend your water feature into the rest of the garden. The moisture lovers will provide a second tier behind the emergent plants, extending the flowering period and enriching the potential for foliage contrasts. Consider the dry ground behind it and you will see what an exuberant bank of foliage can be created at the edge.

planting in water

Gazing into a clear pool is like looking down on a miniature landscape, the colours enhanced by the clarity of the water. With their abundant growth and wide range of foliage textures, the submerged aquatics can create a great variety of beautiful effects. These plants also play a vital role in pond ecology, for they absorb mineral salts and carbon dioxide from the water and release the oxygen necessary to sustain other life. In fine weather, streams of silver oxygen bubbles may be seen rising up from the foliage.

The crowned sovereigns of bottom-rooted plants, whose leaves pattern the surface while at the same time providing shelter for pond life, are the water lilies (*Nymphaea*). These range from miniature cultivars for water 10cm (4in) deep to the giant *N. tuberosa* 'Victoria Longwood', whose spiky, upturned leaves can reach up to 2m (6ft) in diameter – a sensational plant to grow in large pools in hot countries. There are other spectacular tropical varieties worth trying to grow if you live in an area where summers are hot: those that bloom by day tend to have variegated leaves, mottled or striped in green and maroon, and hold up brilliant, many-petalled heads high above the water, while the night-flowering varieties are often sweetly scented and particularly vibrantly coloured.

A huge number of cold-water varieties of nymphaea have been developed since the beginning of the twentieth century – for water ranging from 10cm (4in) to 2m (6ft) in depth. Their colours, petals and leaf shapes vary widely – though there is still none with a flower that is a true blue. These water lilies are easy to grow, requiring only a rich, heavy planting medium and the correct depth of water above the crown, so whether you are working with just a small half-barrel or with a lake, you should be able to include a water lily in your planting scheme, if you so wish.

Similiar in many ways to water lilies, but suitable for hot climates only, are the lotuses. There are varieties for both shallow and deep water, but many, like the sacred lotus

tolerant water hawthorn (*Aponogeton distachyos*) is a superb perennial with glossy green, strap-like leaves and an abundance of scented, pure white flowers at least twice a year, if not throughout the summer. The spatterdock or brandy bottle (*Nuphar*), with its heart-shaped leaves and bright yellow, globular blooms, thrives in cold, shady, even moving water, the Japanese pond lily (*Nuphar japonica*) and yellow pond lily (*N. lutea*) in particular. The wavy underwater leaves of these water lily-like plants are pale and appear almost transparent.

In still, chalky, alkaline ponds grow stoneworts, *Chara vulgaris* and *C. nitella*. These primitive and venerable plants form mounds like pale green clouds seen from above. They are often accompanied by the brighter green domes of water starwort (*Callitriche*), an oxygenator which will grow in still or running water – even in wintry conditions where it will continue to grow underneath the ice. It has long trailing stems which twitch bewitchingly in the current. Another good contrast to the bright green of the callitriche is offered by olive green willow moss (*Fontinalis antipyretica*).

Dappling the water's surface in spring, the white buttercup-like flowers of water crowfoot (*Ranunculus aquatilis*) are an

above: *Smaller types of water lily share the shallows with emergent plants such as bottle brush or mares tail creating an interesting foliage contrast.*

centre: *The golden club (Orontium aquaticum) makes an unusual compact cllump forming subject for the shallows.*

right: *The aquatic plants create a habitat for a wide range of creatures from tiny insects to water fowl.*

opposite: *A wildlife pond should possess a range of plants, and rocks or a landing stage as a shelter for amphibians.*

(*Nelumbo nucifera*) with its exquisite flesh-tinted blooms, are extremely vigorous and may need confining in a planting bay. The leaves at first lie flat, floating on the water, but soon stout stalks raise them clear, resembling parasols.

My favourite underwater plant is hornwort (*Ceratophyllum demersum*). Found nearly all over the world, this attractive and invaluable oxygenator is good for both small and large ponds, and will thrive in deep shady situations if necessary. It grows close to the bottom to form a covering of bushy, dark green foliage but is rarely invasive. Coarser, and more aggressive, the pondweeds (*Elodea*) are nonetheless super oxygenators and very helpful in clearing newly filled ponds. *Elodea canadensis* is daintier than *E. crispa* (now *Lagarosiphon major*), which tends to send out rope-like stems across the surface.

Where the water is too shady, cold or fast-flowing for water lilies to flourish, there are many other attractive flowering plants from which you can choose. The sturdy, cold- and shade-

added attraction to its foliage. You could consider *Ranunculus fluitans* too if you are intending to plant in running water. The delicate spiked *Myriophyllum spicatum* raises small red flowers 2.5–5 cm (1–2in) above the surface. In spring the water violet (*Hottonia palustris*) bears pale lilac flowers that resemble the wildflower lady's smock (*Cardamine pratensis*).

Curled pondweed (*Potamogeton crispus*), whose over-wintering bronze leaves resemble seaweed, will offer a more substantial effect than the submerged species. Floating fairy fern (*Azolla caroliniana*) is a free-floating plant with tiny green leaves that turn bronze in autumn. It is useful in small ponds for providing areas of shade in summer. Although potentially invasive, it is easily scooped off the surface with a net.

The floating green mats often seen covering wild ponds are, in fact, composed of thousands of tiny individual plants called duckweed (*Lemna*). They are often introduced on the feet of visiting waterfowl, but beware when introducing them deliberately into your pool because, although they provide shade and food for fish and wildfowl, they can rapidly choke the surface. However, these plants are easy to remove with a net from small ponds and they make good mulch for the herbaceous border. Ivy-leaved duckweed (*L. trisulca*) is a slower spreader and is probably the one to choose. Even tinier than the lemnas is the floating *Wolffia arrhiza* which is said to be the smallest flowering plant in the world.

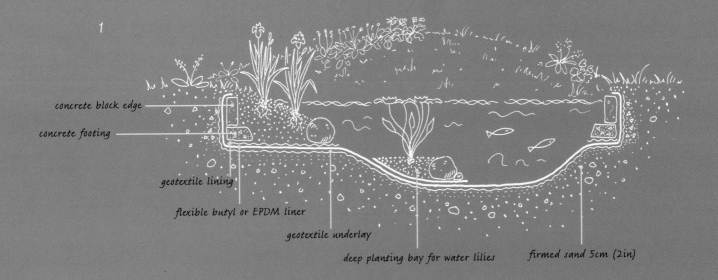

1

concrete block edge

concrete footing

geotextile lining

flexible butyl or EPDM liner

geotextile underlay

deep planting bay for water lilies

firmed sand 5cm (2in)

1 ■ Construction of small naturalistic pond

This fits snugly into a bank of rising ground, gently contoured from the excavated soil. Surrounding the pond is a ledge 25–30cm (10–12in) deep and of varying width. The profile then slopes steeply down to the central area deep enough for water lilies, between 50 and 75cm (20–30in). Once the pond has been excavated, firm and smooth the soil and, if necessary spread a layer of sand over the base and sides.

For an irregular shape it is less wasteful to calculate the area of liner and underlay required if you measure the pond after excavation is complete, by laying a tape measure across the widest and longest points. It is best to line the pond on a warm day when the flexible liner will be softer and easier to handle. Cover the shelves with more geotextile to protect the liner from the concrete footing and blocks that form the edging. Lap the liner over the top of the edging blocks by about 5cm (2in), trim off any excess and backfill with soil or sand. Mortar stones along the edge of the shelf to create planting bays.

2 ■ Alternative edgings for a naturalistic pond
Edge for wildlife

In this example meadow grass butts up to the pond edged with hollow concrete blocks filled with topsoil. A broad mudflat of saturated soil covered with gravel is held back by a row of sandbags or boulders mortared to the shelf edge. Ducks and other birds will be attracted by the water but even more so if cover is provided by a marginal planting of reeds (*Phragmites australis*).

3 ■ Shingle beach

Here the edging blocks are filled with gravel and covered with cobbles and shingle which shelve shallowly down to the water. Grade the stones so the largest ones are nearer the bank. Mortar a row of cobbles to the shelf edge to keep the beach in position.

4 ■ Lawn to water's edge

A hollow concrete block set in a concrete footing and topped up with good quality top soil allows grass to grow right to brink.

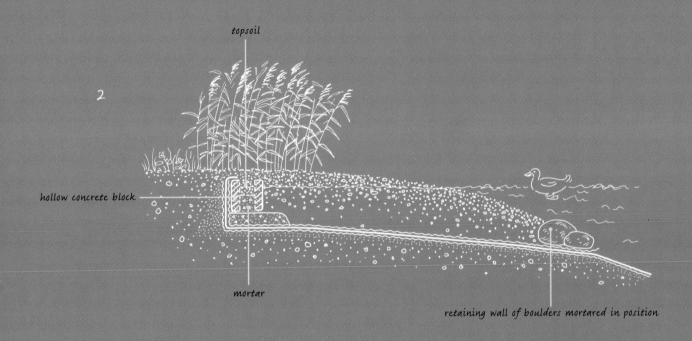

2

topsoil

hollow concrete block

mortar

retaining wall of boulders mortared in position

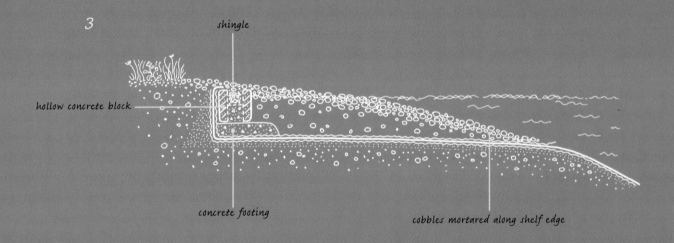

3

shingle

hollow concrete block

concrete footing

cobbles mortared along shelf edge

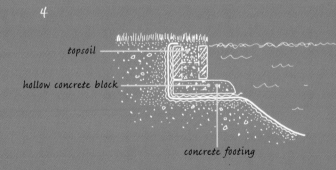

4

topsoil

hollow concrete block

concrete footing

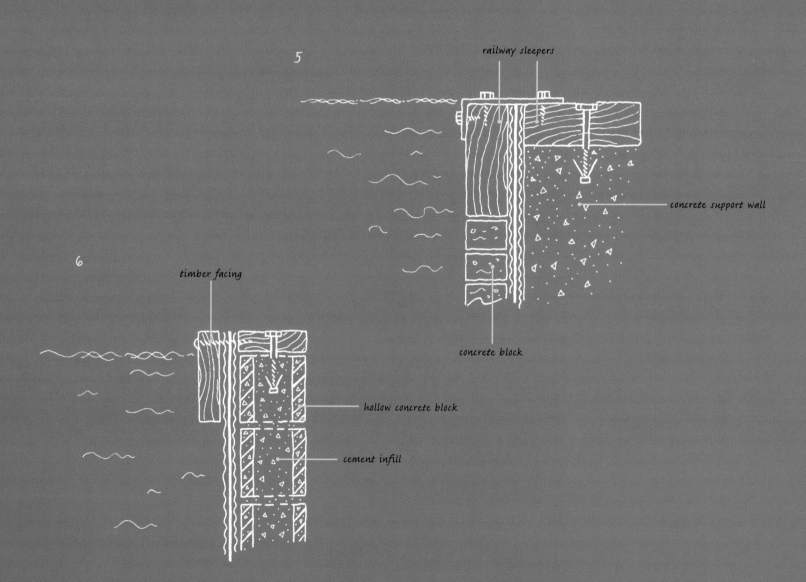

5 ■ *Formal pool edgings*
Timber edge for brimming pool
Railway sleepers form this pool edge, bolted down into the concrete support wall. The geotextile-liner sandwich is held tight against the edge by more sleepers supported on concrete blocks. Cut the liner and geotextile flush with the top before bolting the timbers together by means of a right-angled plate.

6 ■ *Timber edge for a sunken pool*
An edging of hardwood planks is bolted into concrete blocks before the geotextile-liner sandwich is pulled up against the pond side The inner facing is supported temporarily on blocks while it is screwed onto the edging near the top, as the screw will pierce the liner and determine the water level.

5

railway sleepers

concrete support wall

concrete block

6

timber facing

hollow concrete block

cement infill

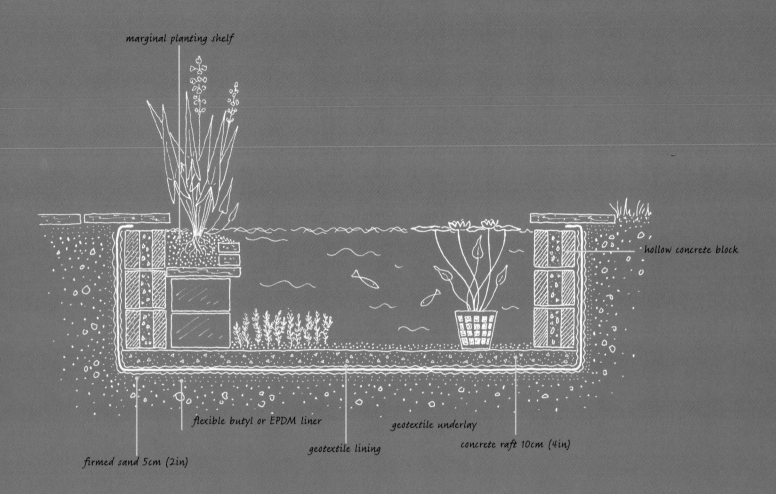

marginal planting shelf

hollow concrete block

flexible butyl or EPDM liner

geotextile underlay

geotextile lining

concrete raft 10cm (4in)

firmed sand 5cm (2in)

7 ■ *Construction of a small formal sunken pool*

Once you have decided on the size of your pool, calculate the amount of liner required by multiplying the length plus twice the depth, by the width plus twice the depth, adding about 30cm (12in) to each figure to allow for overlapping the edge. Excavate the area to a depth of 50–75cm (20–30in) and smooth the surface. Firm a layer of sand over the base and line the pool with geotextile and flexible liner. Over the base spread a raft of concrete and mortar the wall of concrete blocks together tight against the liner. Block piers support a planting shelf about 30cm (12in) wide and no more than 30cm (12in) below the water level. Trim off any excess liner, but leave about 15cm (6in) which is folded over the top of the block walls. An edging of stone slabs is mortared into position over the folded liner. Baskets of newly planted water lilies are first set on bricks so some of the leaves reach the surface, or nearly so. As the plants grow, gradually remove the bricks until the basket sits on the pool floor and the flexible stems are long enough for the leaves to lay flat on the water.

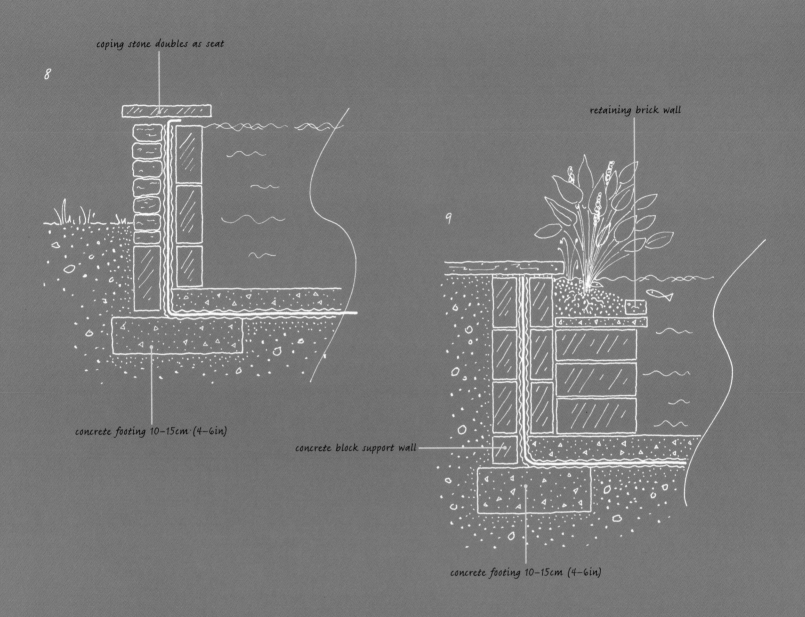

coping stone doubles as seat

8

retaining brick wall

9

concrete footing 10–15cm (4–6in)

concrete block support wall

concrete footing 10–15cm (4–6in)

8 ■ ## Construction of small formal semi-raised pool.

A semi-raised pool is constructed in much the same way as the sunken pool described on page 181. The depth of excavation is much less and concrete footings 10–15cm (4–6in) deep must be prepared to support the walls. In this example the liner runs up between the inner and outer wall and is mortared in position. Above ground level the outer wall is built of stone or brick to give an attractive facing.

9 ■ ## Formal pond planted edge.

The easiest way of siting plants in a formal pond exactly where you want them is to construct simple planting bays. A ledge of paving slabs, no more than 50cm (18in) wide, is raised on concrete blocks 25–30cm (10–12in) below the water level. Good quality topsoil is retained on the ledge by means of a brick wall stopping just below the water's surface.

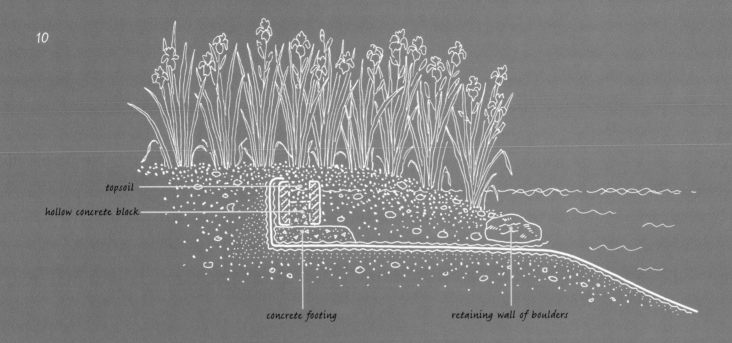

10

topsoil

hollow concrete block

concrete footing

retaining wall of boulders

10 ■ *Informal planted edge*

Many marginal plants enjoy growing in both boggy soil and shallows, so making a transition between the garden and the pond. By establishing planting bays on shelves 25–30cm (10–12in) deep and varying their width you can keep these often vigorous plants in check and achieve a naturalistic effect. Cover the planting ledge with good quality topsoil, sloping the surface down below the waterline to a retaining wall of sandbags or boulders.

In this example land and water merge beneath a drift of irises; the single species is capable of growing in moist soil as well as water. The graduation from dry land to submerged shelf could equally well have been marked by bands of different plants, each growing in their favoured conditions.

WARNING: It is most important to employ a qualified electrician to install an outside power supply. The electricity supply must run in armoured cabling in a rigid plastic pipe buried at least 60cm (24in) below ground level, and a residual current device must be fitted to protect the system.

suppliers list

GENERAL CONSULTANT
Anthony Archer-Wills
Broadford Bridge Road
West Chiltington
West Sussex, RH20 2LF
Tel: 01798 813204

GENERAL CONTRACTORS
Ian Spicer
Inland Waterscapes
Broadford Bridge Road
West Chiltington
West Sussex, RH20 2LF
Tel: 01798 812007

Keir Davidson
13 Waterloo Road
Shepton Mallet
Somerset, BA4 5HG
Tel: 01749 344395

Graduate Gardeners
Calfway Lane
Bisley, Near Stroud
Glos, GL6 7AT
Tel: 01452 770273

GARDEN DESIGNERS
Anthea Gibson
22 Edwardes Square
London, W8 6HE
Tel: 0171 6031457

Georgia Langton
Higher Meerhay Farm
Beaminster
Dorset, DT8 3SB
Tel: 01308 863813

Veronica Adams
Lower Hopton Farm
Stoke Lacey, Bromyard
Hereford, HR7 4HX
Tel: 0885 490294

DRILLERS
Anglia Drilling Services
19 Darby Road
Beccles
Suffolk, NR34 9XX

D.W.Griffiths
Griffiths Water Engineers
Lower Barn
Halwell Southpool
Kingsbridge, Devon

Hydracat Ltd
Reema Road
Belshill
Strathclyde
Scotland, ML4 1RR

STEAM DREDGING
James Lowther
Ramridge Dene
Ramridge
Nr Weyhill, SP11 0QP

DREDGING
PHB Contractors and Plant Hire
Rye Farm
Hollands Lane
Henfield
West Sussex, BN5 9QY
Tel: 01273 493496

Dredging International (UK) Ltd
Marine House
18 Baker Street
Weybridge
Surrey, KT13
Tel: 01932 841336

BRIDGES & TIMBER DECKING
Mike Mathias
M.M.Adronit
Unit 9, The 306 Estate
Broomhill Road
Brislington
Bristol, BS4 5RG
Tel: 0117 9712405

Blenheim Estate Sawmills
Combe
Witney
Oxon, OX8 8ET
Tel: 01993 881206

Armada (UK)
Charlton House
41 Wymondley Road
Hitchin
Hertfordshire
SG4 9PR
Tel: 01462 454770

Stuart Garden Architecture
Burrow Hill Farm
Wiveslicombe
Somerset
TA4 2RN
Tel: 01984 667458

FOUNTAINS & WATER DISPLAYS
Invent Water Treatment Ltd
Dell Road
Shawclough, Rochdale
Lancs, OL12 6BZ
Tel: 01706 359155

Ustigate Ltd
Unit 4,
Norfolk Road Industrial Estate
Gravesend
Kent, DA12 2PS
Tel: 01474 363012

Ford Water Pumping Supplies
49–51 Stratford Road
Birmingham, B11 1PQ
Tel: 0121 7728336

LIGHTING
James Davidson
Outdoor Lighting
North Star
St Mary's Street
Southampton, SO14 1PA
Tel: 01703 227228

BB1 Lighting
23 Parkside
Coventry
West Midlands, CV1 2NE
Tel: 01203 551444

Outdoor Lighting (OLS) Ltd
Unit 3, Kingston Business Centre
Fullers Way South
Chessington
Surrey, KT9 1DQ
Tel: 0181 9742211

LINERS & UNDERLAY
Gordon Low Products Ltd
Dragonfly House
Rookery Road
Wyboston
Beds, MK44 3UG
Tel: 01480 405433

Anthony Archer-Wills Ltd
(See above)

Stapeley Water Gardens Ltd
London Road
Stapeley, Nantwich
Cheshire, CW5 7LH
Tel: 01270 623868

WATER PLANTS
Anthony Archer-Wills
(New Barn Aquatic Nursery)
(See above)

Stapeley Water Gardens Ltd
(See above)

Anglo Aquarium
Strayfield Road
Enfield
Middlesex
EN2 9JE
Tel: 0181 3638548

WATER SCULPTURE
Foliole Fountain Project
6 Park Terrace
Tillington
Petworth
West Sussex
GU28 9AE
Tel: 01798 344114

The Hannah Pescar Sculpture Gallery
Black and White Cottage
Standon Lane
Ockley
Surrey
Tel: 01306 627269

William Pye
The Studio
Rear of 31 Bellevue Road
London SW17 7EF

GENERAL POND FISH & SUPPLIERS
Stapeley Water Gardens Ltd
(See above)

COARSE FISH
Fishers Pond Fishery
Colden Common
Nr Winchester
Hampshire
Tel: 01703 694412

Environment Agency Calverton
Fish Farm
Moore Lane
Calverton
Nottingham
NG14 6FZ
Tel: 01602 663174

Humberside Fisheries
Cleaves Farm
Skerne
Driffield
Yorkshire
Tel: 01377 253613

KOI
Clear Water Koi Direct
Acaster Industrial Estate
Acaster Malbis
York
YO23 2TX
Tel: 01904 705536

Kerei Koi
Maple Farm Nursery Gardens
Moss House Lane
Westby
Nr Kirkham
PR4 3PE
Tel: 01772 685100

TROUT
Duncton Mill Trout Farm
Duncton Mill
Petworth
West Sussex
Tel: 01798 342048
Tel: 01798 342294

D. Wright
Castle Hill Trout Farm
Withiel Florey
Wheddon Cross
Minehead
Somerset
Tel: 01398 7221307

Parkwood Trout Farm
Home Mill
Doddington Lane
Harrietsham
Kent
Tel: 01622 859302

WATERFOWL
The Wildfowl and Wetlands Trust
Mill Road
Arundel
Sussex
BN18 9PB
Tel: 01903 883355
Contact for details of
regional branches.

index

Page numbers in *italics* refer to illustrations.

acknowledgments

The publishers wish to thank the following photographers and organisations for their kind permission to reproduce the following images in this book.

1 Jane Lidz (design: Victor Carrasco, Bornos, Spain); 2 Andrew Lawson (design:James Aldridge); 3 Linny Morris Cunningham; 4–5 Images Colour Library; 6 S & O Mathews; 7 Deni Bown/Oxford Scientfic Films; 8 Colin Monteath/Oxford Scientfic Films; 8–9 left Steve Satushek/The Image Bank; 9 right Albert Arnaud/Still Pictures; 9 centre Heikki Nikki/Oxford Scientfic Films; 11 above left Randy Wells/Sharpshooters/Photonica; 11 above right Tony Arruza/Getty Images; 11 centre left Gerard Soury/Oxford Scientfic Films; 11 below Gary Rogers/Lake Dal, Kashmir, India; 12–13 Carlos Navajas/The Image Bank; 14 Boisvieux/Explorer; 15 Marc Solomon/The Image Bank; 17 above left Perigot/Billaud/Marie Claire Maison; 17 above right Ernst Haas/Getty Images; 17 centre Gary S.Chapman/The Image Bank; 17 below left Walter Looss Jr./The Image Bank; 17 below right Jane Lidz/Hemisphere Park, San Antonio, Texas; 18 above AKG/ Staatsgemaeldesammlungen, Munich/Erich Lessing ('Neptune's Steed' – 1892 by Walter Crane); 18 below 'Fishing' by Brad Holland. 20th Century/Private Collection /Bridgeman Art Library; 19 Fitzwilliam Museum, University of Cambridge /Bridgeman Art Library('Sudden Shower at Ohashi Bridge' at Ataka. From the series '100 Views of Edo', 1857 by Ando and Utagawa Hiroshige); 20 left Successions Picasso/DACS1998 /AKG('Deux Femmes Courant sur la Plage' by Pablo Picasso. Summer 1922); 20 right Copyright Daivd Hockney/AKG('Sunbathers' by David Hockney 1965. Acrylic on Canvas 72"x72"); 21 Private Collection//Bridgeman Art Library('Trouville10' by Ben Tobias 20th Century – Bonhams London); 23 Jane Lidz/Alhambra, Spain; 24 Vivian Russell; 25 above M.Isy–Schwart/The Image Bank; 25 below Clive Nichols/Chateau de Versailles, France; 26 left Peter Cook/View; 26–27 right Jane Lidz/Gardens at Ryoan–Ji, Kyoto, Japan; 28–29 Tom King/The Image Bank; 31 Francisco Ontanon/The Image Bank; 32 Martyn F.Chillmaid/Oxford Scientfic Films; 33 John Heseltine/Sharrow Point, Cornwall; 34 left Herbert Ypma/The Interior Archive; 34–35 Harpur Garden Library (design: Bradley Dyruff, California); 36 left Erica Lennard/Joaquin Sorolla's garden, Madrid; 36–37 right Clive Nichols/Mosses by Thomas Nordstrom & Annika Oskarsson /Rosendal, Sweden (garden design: Julie Toll); 38 Helen Fickling (design: Patrick Watson, South Africa); 39 Gary Rogers; 40 left Hannah Lewis/Living Etc.; 40 above right Helen Fickling/Festival des Jardins de Chaumont-sur-Loire (41), France; 40 below right Michele Lamontagne/Festival des Jardins de Chaumont-sur-Loire (41), France; 41 Clive Nichols/Villa la Casella, France (design: Claus Scheinert); 42 left Herbert Ypma/The Interior Archive; 42–43 main picture Jane Lidz/Church of the Nativity, Rancho Santa Fe, California; 43 right Marion Nickig(artist: Huub Kortekaas, Winssen, Holland; 44 left Jane Lidz/ Alocoa Building, San Francisco(architects: Moore, Rulde, Yudell); 44–45 above centre Infocus International/The Image Bank; 44–45 below centre Helen Fickling/Parc Andre', Citreon, Paris; 45 right Sofia Brignone/Sol Oriente, Careyes, Mexico; 46 Harpur Garden Library (design: Frank Cabot, Quebec, Canada); 46–47 Vivian Russell/Villa Cuzzano, Italy; 48–49 Lorna Rose/Central Garden Home units, Sydney; 50 left Marion Nickig/Quinta Da Bela Vista, Sintra, Portugal; 50 right Harpur Garden Library (design: Thomas Church, San Francisco CA); 51 Harpur Garden Library (design: Bill Wheeler, NY); 52 Kate Zari Roberts/The Garden Picture Library; 53 Harpur Garden Library (design: Topher Delaney, NYC); 55 above right Harpur Garden Library (design: Belt Collins Associates, Hong Kong); 55 above right Gary Rogers/Daily Telegraph garden – RHS Chelsea (design: Arabella Lennox-Boyd); 55 below Hugh Palmer/Badminton; 60–61 Images Colour Library; 63 Images Colour Library; 64 left Michael Melford/The Image Bank; 64–65 centre Steve Satushek/The Image Bank; 65 right John Heseltine; 66–67 Georgia Glynn-Smith/The Garden Picture Library/Kilfane, Kilkenny, Ireland; 68 Andrew Lawson (design: Anthea Gibson); 69 Helen Fickling (design: Patrick Watson, South Africa); 70 above Murray Alcosser/The Image Bank; 70 below Jane Lidz/IBM Westlake, Solana, Texas R&D; 71 Roger Foley; 72 left Nicola Browne/AL Contracts of Weybridge Ltd (design: Andy Sturgeon); 72 above right Stofan Pfander/G+J Fotoservice /Photonica; 72 below right Roger Foley (design: Sheela Lampietti); 73 Grant Faint/The Image Bank; 74–75 Sadao Hibi/NHK publishing Co. Ltd; 76 Fritz von der Schulenburg/ World of Interiors/The Conde Nast Publications Ltd; 77 Reiner Blunck(architect: Luigi Roselli/landscape design: Vladimir Sitta); 78–79 Vincent Motte/Dominique Lafourcade's garden, France; 80 Hugh Palmer/Rousham; 82–83 main picture Gary Rogers/Chatsworth Estate; 83 left & right Helen Fickling/Festival des Jardins de Chaumont-sur-Loire (41), France; 84–85 Vivian Russell; 86 Sadao Hibi/NHK Publishing Co. td; 87 left Andrew Lawson; 87 right Sadao Hibi/NHK Publishing Co. Ltd; 89 Antony Archer-Wills; 90 left Simon McBride/Ninfa,Italy; 90–91 centre Andrew Lawson; 91 right Jonathan Buckley (design: John Tordoff); 92 left Koji Nakamura/Photonica; 92–93 main picture Roger Foley; 98–99 Images Colour Library; 101 Simon Fraser; 102 Simon Fraser ; 102–103 inset John W. Banagan/The Image Bank; 103 right James H. Carmichael JR.

/The Image Bank; 103 centre S & O Mathews; 104–105 Tim Street-Porter (design: Luis Barragan); 106 left Trevor Mein/Belle Magazine; 106–107 centre Gary Rogers /Council for a beautiful Israel/RHS Chelsea (design: Professor David Stevens); 107 right Roger Foley (design: Osamu Shimizu); 108 above Roger Foley (design: Oehme, van Sweden and Assoc.); 108 below Gary Rogers/Meinhard garden, Germany (design: Henk Weijers); 109 left MAP/Mise Au Point– NOUN'; 109 right Roger Foley/Pollack Garden; 110 Roger Foley (design: Ellen Penick); 112 left Herbert Ypma/The Interior Archive; 112–113 main picture Jane Lidz/IBM Irvine, California (design: Peter Walker); 113 right Andrew Lawson (design: James Aldridge); 114 Harpur Garden Library (design: Mel Light LA, California); 115 right Charles Mann(architect: Steve); 115 above left Andrew Lawson/RHS Chelsea (design: Christopher Bradley-Hole); 115 below left Mick Hales/Green World Picture; 116 Michele Lamontagne/Cords sur Ceil, France; 117 Neil Campbell-Sharp/Powerscourt, Co. Wicklow. Ireland; 118 left Herbert Ypma/The Interior Archive; 118–119 centre Mori Toyofumi/The Image Bank; 119 right Jane Lidz /Walnut Creek, California. 101 Ignacio(architect: George Meirs); 120 left Nicola Browne; 120–121 centre Jane Lidz/San Bayhill, Matco, California; 121 right Jane Lidz; 122 Harpur Garden Library (design: Oheme, van Sweden and Assoc); 123 left Anne Hyde/The Dorothy Clive garden, Staffordshire; 123 above right Kaz Mori/The Image Bank; 123 below right S & O Mathews; 128–129 Images Colour Library; 131 Joanna McCarthy/The Image Bank; 132 John Heseltine; 132–133 Harold Taylor ABIPP/Oxford Scientific Films; 133 S&O Mathews; 134–135 D.Zintzmeyer/Image du Sud; 136 left Harpur Garden Library (design: Little & Lewis, Washington); 136–137 main picture Roger Foley (design: Oehme, van Sweden and Assoc); 138 left Marianne Majerus (design: Charles Jencks); 138 above right Andrew Lawson (design: James Aldridge); 138 below right Christian Sarramon/Miojo Careyes, Mexico; 139 right Herbert Ypma/The Interior Archive; 139 main picture Tim Street-Porter/Vidal Sasson's House LA(architect: Larry Totah); 140 left Roger Foley (design: Oehme, van Sweden and Assoc); 140–141 centre Roger Foley (design: Oehme van Sweden and Assc); 141 right Andrew Lawson/Stone Lane Gardens, Chagford, Devon; 142 left Gil Hanly/Ivan Nagel's garden (design: Gary Boyle); 142 right Harpur Garden Library (design: Frank Cabot, NY); 143 Marianne Majerus; 144 Roger Foley (design: Oehme, van Sweden and Assoc); 145 Roger Foley (design: Oehme, van Sweden and Assc); 146 Reiner Blunck /Diener(architect: Luigi Snozzi); 147 Le Studio/Image du Sud;

148 left Ingalill Snitt; 148–149 right Earl Carter/Belle-Arcaid; 149 left Reiner Blunck/Arcaid/Adelphi Hotel, Melbourne, Australia(architect: Denton Corker Marshall); 149 above right Roger Foley; 149 below right Reiner Blunck/Arcaid/Adelphi Hotel Melbourne, Australia (architect: Denton Corker Marshall); 150 Harpur Garden Library/Dynasty Court, HK (design: Belt Collins Associates, Hong Kong); 151 Pascal Chevallier/Agence Top; 152 left Roger Foley (design: Florence Everts); 152–153 main picture Helen Fickling/Qua Zulu Natal, South Africa; 154 left Harpur Garden Library (design: Arthur Erickson, Vancouver, Canada); 154 right Harpur Garden Library (design: Topher Delany, San Francisco); 155 left Edina Van der Wyck/The Interior Archive; 155 right Gary Rogers/Goa Inc/RHS Chelsea (design: Hiroshi Nanamori); 156–157 Richard Bryant/Arcaid(architect: Astrid Lohss); 158 left Andrew Lawson; 158 right Steve Satushek/The Image Bank; 159 left T.Yamaguchi/Photonica; 159 right Andrea Pistolesi/The Image Bank; 160 Undine Prohl(architect: Jose de Yturbe, Mexico); 161 Reiner Blunck(architect: Glenn Murcutt); 162 left Undine Prohl(architects: Legorreta Arquitectos, Mexico); 162–163 main picture Undine Prohl(architects: Legorreta Arquitectos, Mexico); 163 right Undine Prohl(architect: Enrique Norten, Mexico); 164 Leigh Clapp (design: Michael Cooke)/Hawthorne Stud, NSW, Australia; 165 Alfred Wolf; 166 Harpur Garden Library (design: Mr and Mrs Lerner, California); 167 Reiner Blunck(architect: Mathias Hoffmann); 168–169 Marianne Majerus/Beth Chatto's garden, Essex; 170 left S & O Mathews; 170 main picture Roger Foley (design: Oehme van Sweden and Assoc); 171 left Roger Foley(design: Oehme, van Sweden and Assoc); 171 right Nicola Browne/The Menagerie, Northamptonshire; 173 Linny Morris Cunningham; 174 left Ursel Borstell; 174 centre S & O Mathews; 174–175 centre right Laurence Hughes/The Image Bank; 175 above right Gary Rogers; 175 below right Hans Reinhard/Oxford Scientfic Films; 176–177 Lena Ehrenstrom /Naturbild, Stockholm; 184 Images Colour Library; 185 Gary Cralle/The Image Bank; 186–187 Images Colour Library; 188–189 Images Colour Library; 191 Linny Morris Cunningham; 192 Rene Burri/Magnum Photos,London.

Endpapers Images Colour Library

publisher's acknowledgments
The publisher would like to thank Barbara Haynes and Leslie Craig for all their hard work, and Olivia Norton for assistance with typesetting.

author's acknowledgments

I must first begin by thanking Stuart Cooper of Conran Octopus for asking me to write this book in the first place. Perhaps he was beguiled by my enthusiastic chatter about waterfalls of exuberance and unusual complexity, or maybe by the curious escapades I have had during my lifetime with water. Next, I would like to thank the Nash family for all their help and support particularly at the beginning stages of the project. My good friend David Rathbun deserves special appreciation for his extraordinary insight and artistry in landscape design which I found so exciting. Thanks, also, to James Laurice and all my friends in America who have been so hospitable and supportive.

My gratitude must also go to all the wonderful clients and customers who have called me to their gardens and estates to advise or help with the many diverse water features which I have pictured in my mind during the initial writing.

A big thank you and a round of applause must go to Gail Patterson for all her typing and retyping of this book. Also, I would like to thank my daughter Catherine for her efforts on the computer. However, my greatest thanks must undoubtedly go to my wife Lynn for the hundreds of hours she spent researching and checking historic and artistic details, and for all her help and support with the writing of this book.